POETRY

Also by Raymond Carver

FICTION

Will You Please Be Quiet, Please?
Furious Seasons
What We Talk About When We Talk About Love
Cathedral
Where I'm Calling From

POETRY

Winter Insomnia
At Night the Salmon Move
Where Water Comes Together with Other Water
Ultramarine

PROSE AND POETRY

Fires

A NEW PATH
TO THE
WATERFALL

A NEW PATH TO THE WATERFALL

POEMS

Raymond Carver

INTRODUCTION BY
TESS GALLAGHER

*for Edith Lippert —
in appreciation for your love
of books & of learning.
very best.*

*Tess Gallagher
Carver*

THE ATLANTIC MONTHLY PRESS
NEW YORK

•

*May 21, 1989
Pt. Angeles*

Copyright © 1989 by the estate of Raymond Carver
Introduction copyright © 1989 by Tess Gallagher
A list of acknowledgments and permissions appears on pp. 123–24

Published simultaneously in Canada
Printed in the United States of America

Library of Congress Cataloging-in-Publication Data

Carver, Raymond.
   A new path to the waterfall.

   I. Title.
PS3553.A7894N48   1989   811'.54   88-34989
ISBN 0-87113-280-X
ISBN 0-87113-301-6 (deluxe)

Design by Laura Hough

Endpapers: *The Hero's Journey* by Alfredo Arreguin

The Atlantic Monthly Press
19 Union Square West
New York, NY 10003

FIRST PRINTING

Tess. Tess. Tess. Tess

GIFT

A day so happy.
Fog lifted early, I worked in the garden.
Hummingbirds were stopping over honeysuckle flowers.
There was no thing on earth I wanted to possess.
I knew no one worth my envying him.
Whatever evil I had suffered, I forgot.
To think that once I was the same man did not embarrass me.
In my body I felt no pain.
When straightening up, I saw the blue sea and sails.

—Czeslaw Milosz

CONTENTS

INTRODUCTION

This is a last book and last things, as we learn, have rights of their own. They don't need us, but in our need of them we commemorate and make more real that finality which encircles us, and draws us again into that central question of any death: What is life for? Raymond Carver lived and wrote his answer: "I've always squandered," he told an interviewer, no doubt steering a hard course away from the lofty and noble. It was almost a law, Carver's law, not to save up things for some longed-for future, but to use up the best that was in him each day and to trust that more would come. Even the packaging of the cigarettes he smoked bore the imprint of his oath in the imperative: NOW.

This was an injunction that would bear down on us with increasing intensity as we attempted to finish this book. In an episode eerily like that which preceded the death of Chekhov, to whom he had recently paid tribute in his story "Errand," Ray had been diagnosed with lung cancer after spitting up blood in September 1987. There would follow ten months of struggle during which the cancer would reoccur as a brain tumor in early March. After twice swerving away from recommendations for brain surgery by several doctors, he would undergo seven weeks of intense, full-brain radiation. After a short respite, however, tumors would again be found in his lungs in early June.

These are the facts of that time, enough to have made realists out of us if we hadn't been realists already. Nonetheless, much as Chekhov had kept reading the train schedules away from the town in which he would die, Ray kept working, planning, believing in the importance of the time he had left, and also believing that he might, through some loop in fate, even get out of this. An errand list I found in his shirt pocket later read "eggs, peanut butter, hot choc" and then, after a space, "Australia? Antarctica??" The insistent nature of Ray's belief in his own capacity to recover from reversals during the course of his illness gave us both strength. In his journal he wrote: "When hope is gone, the ultimate sanity is to grasp at straws." In this way he lived hope as a function of gesture, a reaching for or toward, while the object of promise stayed rightly illusory. The alternative was acceptance of death, which at age fifty was impossible for him. Another journal entry revealed his anguish as the pace of the disease quickened: "I wish I had a while. Not five years—or even three years—I couldn't ask for that long, but if I had even a year. If I knew I had a year."

In January 1988 Ray began keeping a journal under the inspiration of Stephen Spender's *Journals/1939–1983*, but with the discovery of his brain tumor it broke off suddenly in March, though he would start again in another notebook later. Our attentions were turned instead to the task of drafting a short essay to appear in the commencement booklet for the University of Hartford, where Ray was to accept a Doctorate of Letters in May.

During much of this time I had been clinging to the stories of Chekhov, reading one after the other of the Ecco Press volumes, and now I offered two passages to Ray from *Ward No. 6* to illustrate the epigraph from Saint Teresa ("Words lead to deeds . . . they prepare the soul, make it ready, and move it to tenderness"), which he'd used from my book of poems to begin his essay. Ray incorporated the passages from Chekhov into his piece, and this was the beginning of an important spiritual accompaniment which began to run through our days, and which eventually would play an important part in the writing of this book.

The fervor with which we both seized on these particular moments in *Ward No. 6* came, I think, directly out of the ordeal we were undergoing with Ray's health, and this was particularly true of the second passage in which two characters, a disaffected doctor and an imperious postmaster, his elder, suddenly find themselves discussing the human soul:

> "*And you do not believe in the immortality of the soul?*"
> "*No, honored Mihail Averyanitch; I do not believe it, and, have no grounds for believing it.*"
> "*I must own I doubt it too,*" Mihail Averyanitch admits. "*And yet I have a feeling as though I should never die myself: 'Old fogey, it's time you were dead!' but there is a little voice in my soul that says: 'Don't believe it; you won't die.'*"

In his framing of the passage Ray underscored the power of "words which linger as deeds" and out of which "a little voice in the soul" is born. He seemed almost grateful to observe how in the Chekhov story "the way we have dismissed certain concepts about life, about death, suddenly gives over unexpectedly to belief of an admittedly fragile but insistent nature."

I continued to bring Chekhov into our days by reading a story first thing in the morning and then telling it to Ray when I came down for breakfast. I would give the story in as true a fashion as I could, and Ray would inevitably become engaged by it and have to read it for himself that afternoon. By evening we could discuss it.

Another of Ray's influences came from one of the books he'd been reading early in the year, Czeslaw Milosz's *Unattainable Earth,* and it began to affect his idea of the form and latitude his own book might discover. In the interests of what he called "a more spacious form," Milosz had incorporated prose quotes from Casanova's *Memoirs,* snippets from Baudelaire, from his uncle Oscar Milosz, Pascal, Goethe and other thinkers and writers who'd affected him as he was writing his poems. He also includes his own musings, which take the form of confessions, questionings and insights. Ray was very much attracted to the inclusiveness of Milosz's approach. His own reading at the time included García Lorca, Jaroslav Seifert, Tomas Tranströmer, Lowell, *The Selected Poems* of Milosz and a rereading of Tolstoy's *The Death of Ivan Ilych*. From these he selected whole poems, which we later used as section heads for the book.

But in early June, when the devastating news of tumors in the lungs again was given to us, it was to Chekhov we instinctively turned to restore our steadfastness. One night I looked at certain passages I had bracketed in the stories and realized that they seemed to be speaking toward poems of Ray's which I'd been helping him revise and typing into the computer. On impulse I went to the typewriter and shaped some of these excerpts into lines and gave them titles. When I showed the results to Ray, it was as if we'd discovered another Chekhov inside Chekhov. But because I'd been looking at the passages with Ray's poems in mind, there was the sense that Chekhov had stepped toward us, and that while he remained in his own time, he seemed also to have become our contemporary. The world of headlong carriage races through snowstorms and of herring-head soup, of a dish made of bulls' eyes, of cooks picking sorrel for vegetable soup, of peasant children raised not to flinch at the crude language of their drunken parents—this world was at home with the world of Raymond Carver, in which a man puts his head on the executioner's block while touring a castle only to have the hand of his companion come down on his neck like an axe, a world in which a drunken father is caught in the kitchen by his son with a strange woman in a heavily sexual context, and in which we watch as a drowned child is carried above the trees in the tongs of a helicopter.

Once we'd discovered the poet in Chekhov, Ray began to mark passages he wanted to include and to type them up himself. The results were something between poems and prose, and this pleased us because some of Ray's new poems blurred the boundaries between poem and story, just as his stories had often taken strength from dramatic and poetic strategies. Ray had so collapsed the distance between his language and thought that the resulting transparency of method allowed distinctions between genres to dissolve without violence or a feeling of trespass. The story given as poem could unwind without having to pretend to intensities of phrasing or language that might have impeded the force of the story itself, yet the story could pull at the attention of the reader in another way for having been conceived as poetry.

In order to work at all on the book during what was a bewildering time for us, we made the decision not to tell anyone about the cancer's recurrence in the lungs. Instead of giving over to visitors and a parade of sorrowful goodbyes we could keep our attention on the things we wanted to do. And one of the things we decided to do was to celebrate our eleven years together by getting married in Reno, Nevada, on June 17. The wedding was what Ray called a "high tacky affair" and it took place across from the courthouse in the Heart of Reno Chapel, which had a huge heart in the window spiked with small golden light bulbs and a sign that read SE HABLA ESPANOL. Afterwards we went gambling in the casinos and I headed into a phenomenal three-day winning streak at roulette.

When we returned home Ray wrote "Proposal," which carries the urgency of that time, the raw sense of life lived without guile, or that cushion of hope we count on to extend life past the provisional. Our having married anchored us in a new way and it seemed we had knowingly saved this occasion to give ourselves solace, and perhaps also to allow us to toss back our heads once more in a rippling cosmic laugh as from that "gay and empty journey" Kafka writes of.

This was also the time during which Ray wrote "Gravy." The idea for the poem had come from a conversation we'd had while sitting on the deck facing the Strait of Juan de Fuca, taking stock. "You remember telling me how you almost died before you met me?" I asked him. "It could've ended back then and we'd never even have met. None of this would have happened." We sat there quietly, just marveling at what we'd been allowed. "It's all been gravy," Ray said. "Pure gravy."

Many of the poems Ray had accumulated toward the book had been drafted during July and late August the summer before. Nearly a year later, in early July, enough finished poems had accumulated that we decided I should begin to arrange them into sections and to shape the book. I had done this with each of Ray's collections of poetry and also with most of his fiction. My perhaps primitive way of ordering a manuscript was to scatter the pages out on the living-room floor and crawl on my hands and knees among them, reading and sensing what should come next, moving by intuition and story and emotion.

We had decided to try to include the Chekhov passages. The stories had been so integral to our spiritual survival that, as with Milosz's inclusion of Whitman in his book, Chekhov seemed a companion-soul, as if Ray had somehow won permission through a lifetime of admiration to take up his work with the audacity of love.

One night I remember watching with Ray a composer being interviewed on television, and the composer was exclaiming that Tchaikovsky had lifted whole passages from Beethoven and offered them as his own. When someone had challenged him about this he had said simply, "I have a right. I love him." Ray had jotted down this exchange, and I think this right-of-love figured heavily into his decision to bring Chekhov so boldly into conjunction with his own work. The Chekhov passages also bound Ray's poetry to his fiction, his last collection having ended with the tribute of "Errand." The Chekhov selections seemed to fall very naturally into place in the manuscript, keying and amplifying in a tonal and emotional way the poems Ray had been writing. At times, through Chekhov, Ray was able to give himself and others instructions for the difficult task of continuing under the certainty of loss ("Downstream"), or he could admit fears he might have stifled in order to keep the upper hand in his waiting game with cancer ("Foreboding" and "Sparrow Nights").

The book, as we finalized my arrangement, fell into six sections. It began with poems retrieved from earlier publications, poems which, for one reason and another, had not been joined with more recent work. So just as Ray was bringing the time of Chekhov to bear on his work, he was carrying forward poems from his earlier life, and perhaps affecting both lives in their imaginative composition. I think in this regard that a passage he had marked in Milosz's *Unattainable Earth* may illuminate Ray's inner objectives:

Jeanne, a disciple of Karl Jaspers, taught me the philosophy of freedom, which consists in being aware that a choice made now, today, projects itself backwards and changes our past actions.

There was an urge in Ray's writing, in both the poems and stories, to revisit certain evocative scenes and characters in his life, to wrest from them if not release, then at least a telling anatomy of the occasion. In this book the early love poems hint at a dark element which is realized more fully in recent poems such as "Miracle," "The Offending Eel" and "Wake Up." The son as an oppressive figure in former poems and in the stories "Elephant" and "The Compartment" reappears in "On an Old Photograph of My Son," and although the pain is freshly present, there is the redeeming knowledge at the end of the poem that "we all do better in the future." The theme of the dead child, which was explored so poignantly in his story "A Small, Good Thing" is revived in the poem "Lemonade," in which a child, sent by the father for a thermos of lemonade, drowns in the river.

The second section introduced a series of poems whose territory was suggested by Tomas Tranströmer's poem, "The Name," about a loss of identity. Perhaps the best way to characterize these poems is by their dis-ease, the way in which a wildness, a strangeness, can erupt and carry us into realms of unreason with no way to turn back. Here the verbally abusive woman of his story "Intimacy" is joined by the physically abusive woman of "Miracle." Drinking continued to motivate the rituals of disintegration in the poems about his first marriage, and he inventoried the havoc it had caused as if it had occurred only yesterday.

Childhood innocence is abruptly sundered in the third section with "The Kitchen," which recalls the story "Nobody Said Anything." There are poems in which the unknown is left fully intact, as in "The Sturgeon" and "Another Mystery." The violence of working-class family life in "Suspenders" plays off a section from Chekhov about peasant life and the brutalizing of the sensibilities of children.

The hard question Milosz asks in "Return to Kraków in 1880" at the front of the fourth section—"To win? To lose?/What for, if the world will forget us anyway?"—challenges the poet's sense of memory as an entrustment. And for Ray, of course, in facing his death the idea of whether one's memory would persist importantly in the survival of one's writing was also present. His poems suggest that an artist's obsessions and signs, fragmentary and intermittent as they may be, exist in a world of necessity that transcends anyone else's need of them. At the same time, poems like "One More" and "His Bathrobe Pockets Stuffed with Notes" reveal humorously the haphazard nature of creation itself, and indeed the amazement that anything worthwhile should accumulate from such a scattershot process. There is also a prose record in this section of Ray's first intimations of the literary life when he's handed a copy of *Poetry* by an elderly man whose home he enters as a delivery boy. Here, as in "Errand," it is the ordinary moment which illuminates the most extraordinary things. A magazine passes from one hand to another and the young would-be writer discovers, to his surprise, a world in which writing and reading poems is believed to be a creditable endeavor.

The juxtaposition of contemporary time with the era of knights and chivalry in "The Offending Eel" is one we've seen before in the story "What We Talk About When We Talk About Love," and also in the more recent "Blackbird Pie." Such counterpointing seems to allow the contemporary material a fresh barbarism. In light of the Lowell quote that begins the fifth section—"Yet why not say what happened?"—we look with fluorescent starkness into the unrelenting, obsessive magnetism of "the real," its traps and violences.

The poem "Summer Fog" in the same section was made all the more extraordinary for me because of something Ray said when he first gave me the poem to read. He told me he was sorry he wouldn't be there to do the things for me that I was doing for him. "I've tried something here," he said. "I don't know if it works." What he had tried was to leap ahead into the time of my death, and to imagine his grief as a gift to me against my own approaching solitude. It seems all the more moving that this was done at a time when his own death was, in the words of the poem, the "stupendous grief" we were feeling together.

The last section of the book deals with the stages of his awareness as his health worsened and he moved toward death. In "Gravy," as I've mentioned, he displaces the devastating significance of death in the present by inserting the memory of a prior death narrowly avoided, when in 1976–77 he had nearly died of alcoholism. So in effect he uses his coming death as proof of a former escape; and death, he realized, once displaced by such an excess of living during the ten productive years he'd been allowed, could never be quite the same. Nevertheless, the introductory passages from Chekhov ("Foreboding" and "Sparrow Nights") acknowledge an inner panic. Along with the matter-of-factness of "What the Doctor Said" and the "practicing" for death in "Wake Up," there is the defiance of "Proposal," and the two poems which rehearse the final goodbye—"No Need" and "Through the Boughs." I hadn't realized until three weeks after Ray's death, as I went over the manuscript to enter corrections Ray had made before we'd taken the final trip to Alaska, that I had perfectly, though unwittingly, enacted the instructions of "No Need" the night before his death. The three kisses which had been meant as "Good night" had, at the time, carried the possibility that Ray would not wake again. "Don't be afraid," I'd said. "Just go into your sleep now" and, finally, "I love you"—to which he had answered, "I love you too. You get some sleep now." He never opened his eyes again, and at 6:20 the next morning he stopped breathing.

The "jaunty" slant of the cigarette in the self-portrait "After-glow" belies the consequences which have made this a last glance. Maybe it's as close as Ray would let himself come to irony at a time when a lesser writer might have carved out a sad, edgy little empire with it. In the final poem, "Late Fragment," the voice has earned a more elevated coda. There is the sense that central to the effort of the life, of the writing, has been the need to be beloved and that one's own willingness to award that to the self—to "call myself beloved" and, beyond that, to "feel myself beloved on the earth"—has somehow been achieved. For a recovering alcoholic, this self-recognition and the more generalized feeling of love he was allowing himself was no small accomplishment. Ray knew he had been graced and blessed and that his writing had enabled him to reach far beyond the often mean circumstances from which he and those he wrote about had come, and also that through his writing those working-class lives had become a part of literature. On a piece of scrap paper near his typewriter he had written: "Forgive me if I'm thrilled with the idea, but just now I thought that every poem I write ought to be called 'Happiness.'" And he was, in spite of not agreeing to such an early death, in the keeping of a grateful equanimity when we talked during those long summer evenings of what our life together as writers, lovers and helpmates had been.

By mid-July his last book was finished and I had found its title, taken from an early poem called "Looking for Work." We didn't discuss the title; we just knew it was right. We had been given a rather incredible gift shortly after our wedding and this, I think, influenced us in our choice. Our painter friend, Alfredo Arreguin, had been working on a large painting about which mysterious, tantalizing hints had been leaked at intervals to us by his wife, Susan Lytle, also a painter. The day before our wedding reception, Alfredo and Susan arrived with the painting strapped to the top of their car. The painting, once hung in our living room, proved to be of several salmon leaping midair toward a vigorous, stylized waterfall. In the sky, what Ray would call "the ghost fish" were patterned into clouds heading in the opposite direction. The rocks in the background were inhabited as well, studded with prehistoric eyes.

Each morning we took our coffee in front of the painting where Ray could sometimes be seen sitting alone during the day, meditating. When I look at it now, his particular aliveness seems imbedded there in the pageantry of a cycle we had seen played out year after year in the river below our house. In the painting the fish are heading upstream, bowed eternally to the light in a fierce, determined flight above water, and above them the ghost fish float unimpeded in an opposing current, relieved of their struggle.

In Alaska, on one last fishing trip, we raised glasses of Perrier to toast the book, and ourselves, for having managed to finish it against so many odds. In the crucial last days of our work, guests had arrived for an extended stay and Ray's son had come from Germany. We'd kept working, parceling out the day, until the work was done. "Don't tell them we've finished," he said to me—"them" meaning the guests. "I need you here." So the book as pretext allowed us a few more precious mornings with each other before what would be the final onset of his illness. After our guests had left, we began making calls, trying desperately to arrange a trip to Russia to see Chekhov's grave and to visit the houses of Dostoyevski and Tolstoy. There were places associated with Akhmatova that I wanted to find. Even though this wasn't to be, our planning in those last days was, in itself, a kind of dream-visit that lifted our spirits. Later, when Ray entered the hospital, we talked about what a great trip it would have been. "I'll go there,"

I said, "I'll go for us." "I'll get there before you," he said, and grinned. "I'm traveling faster."

After Ray's death at home in Port Angeles on August 2, the mail was heaped for weeks with letters and cards from people all over the world mourning his passing, sending me often very moving accounts of their having met him even briefly, things he'd said, acts of kindness performed, stories of his life before I had known him. Copies of obituaries also began to arrive from papers around the country, and one day I opened a packet from London with the obituary from the *Sunday Times*. The headline above the photograph of Ray with his hands in his jacket pocket reads simply: "The American Chekhov." From *The Guardian* there was the possessive "America's Chekhov." I seemed to be reading these *with* Ray, and to be carrying his knowing of it. Either headline would have been accolade enough to have made him humbly and deeply happy.

It seems important finally to say that Ray did not regard his poetry as simply a hobby or a pastime he turned to when he wanted a rest from fiction. Poetry was a spiritual necessity. The truths he came to through his poetry involved a dismantling of artifice to a degree not even Williams, whom he had admired early on, could have anticipated. He'd read Milosz's lines in *"Ars Poetica?"* and they'd appealed to him:

> *I have always aspired to a more spacious form*
> *that would be free from the claims of poetry or prose*
> *and would let us understand each other without exposing*
> *the author or reader to sublime agonies.*
>
> *In the very essence of poetry there is something indecent:*
> *a thing is brought forth which we didn't know we had in us,*

so we blink our eyes, as if a tiger had sprung out
and stood in the light, lashing his tail.

Ray used his poetry to flush the tiger from hiding. Further, he did not
look on his writing life as the offering of products to a readership, and
he was purposefully disobedient when pressures were put on him to
write stories because that's where his reputation was centered and that's
where the largest reward in terms of publication and audience lay. He
didn't care. When he received the Mildred and Harold Strauss Living
Award, given only to prose writers, he immediately sat down and
wrote two books of poetry. He was not "building a career"; he was
living a vocation and this meant that his writing, whether poetry or
prose, was tied to inner mandates that insisted more and more on an
increasingly unmediated apprehension of his subjects, and poetry was
the form that best allowed this.

I can imagine that it might be tempting for those who loved
Ray's fiction to the exclusion of his poetry to feel he had gone astray
in giving so much of his time to poetry in the final years. But this
would be to miss the gift of freshness his poems offer in a passionless
era. Because judgments about the contribution of poets lags far behind
those volunteered toward fiction writers in this country, it will likely
be some time before Ray's impact as a poet can be adequately assessed.
So far, the most astute essay on his poetry is Greg Kuzma's, published
in the *Michigan Quarterly Review* (Spring 1988). It could be that Ray,
in his own fashion, has done as much to challenge the idea of what
poetry can be as he did to reinvigorate the short story. What is sure
is that he wrote and lived his last ten years by his own design, and as
his companion in that life, I'm glad to have helped him keep his poetry

alive for the journey, for the comfort and soul making he drew from it so crucially in his too-early going.

—TESS GALLAGHER

A NEW PATH
TO THE
WATERFALL

I

WET PICTURE

Those beautiful days
when the city resembles a die, a fan and a bird song
or a scallop shell on the seashore
> *—goodbye, goodbye, pretty girls,*
> *we met today*
> *and will not ever meet again.*

The beautiful Sundays
when the city resembles a football, a card and an ocarina
or a swinging bell
> *—in the sunny street*
> *the shadows of passers-by were kissing*
> *and people walked away, total strangers.*

Those beautiful evenings
when the city resembles a rose, a chessboard, a violin
or a crying girl
> *—we played dominoes,*
> *black-dotted dominoes with the thin girls in the bar,*
> *watching their knees,*

> *which were emaciated*
> *like two skulls with the silk crowns of their garters*
> *in the desperate kingdom of love.*

—JAROSLAV SEIFERT
(translated by Ewald Osers)

THERMOPYLAE

Back at the hotel, watching her loosen, then comb out
her russet hair in front of the window, she deep in private thought,
her eyes somewhere else, I am reminded for some reason of those
Lacedaemonians Herodotus wrote about, whose duty
it was to hold the Gates against the Persian army. And who
did. For four days. First, though, under the disbelieving
eyes of Xerxes himself, the Greek soldiers sprawled as if
uncaring, outside their timber-hewn walls, arms stacked,
combing and combing their long hair, as if it were
simply another day in an otherwise unremarkable campaign.
When Xerxes demanded to know what such display signified,
he was told, *When these men are about to leave their lives
they first make their heads beautiful.*

      She lays down her bone-handle comb and moves closer
to the window and the mean afternoon light. Something, some
creaking movement from below, has caught her
attention. A look, and it lets her go.

TWO WORLDS

In air heavy
with odor of crocuses,

sensual smell of crocuses,
I watch a lemon sun disappear,

a sea change blue
to olive black.

I watch lightning leap from Asia as
sleeping,

my love stirs and breathes and
sleeps again,

part of this world and yet
part that.

SMOKE AND DECEPTION

*When after supper Tatyana Ivanovna sat quietly down
and took up her knitting, he kept his eyes fixed on her
fingers and chatted away without ceasing.*

*"Make all the haste you can to live, my friends . . ." he said.
"God forbid you should sacrifice the present for the future!
There is youth, health, fire in the present; the future is smoke
and deception! As soon as you are twenty,
begin to live."*

Tatyana Ivanovna dropped a knitting-needle.

—ANTON CHEKHOV
"The Privy Councillor"

IN A GREEK ORTHODOX
CHURCH NEAR DAPHNE

Christ broods over our heads
as you comment on this, on that.
Your voice
is borne through those empty chambers still.

Halt with desire, I follow
outside where we wonderingly examine
ruined walls. Wind
rises to meet the evening.

Wind, you're much overdue.
Wind, let me touch you.
Evening, you've been expected all day.
Evening, hold us and cover us.

And evening sinks down at last.
And wind runs to the four corners of the body.
And walls are gone.
And Christ broods over our heads.

FOR THE RECORD

The papal nuncio, John Burchard, writes calmly
that dozens of mares and stallions
were driven into a courtyard of the Vatican
so the Pope Alexander VI and his daughter,
Lucretia Borgia, could watch from a balcony
"with pleasure and much laughter"
the equine coupling going on below.
When this spectacle was over
they refreshed themselves, then waited
while Lucretia's brother, Caesar,
shot down ten unarmed criminals
who were herded into the same courtyard.
Remember this the next time you see
the name *Borgia,* or the word *Renaissance.*
I don't know what I can make of this,
this morning. I'll leave it for now.
Go for that walk I planned earlier, hope maybe
to see those two herons sift down the cliffside
as they did for us earlier in the season
so we felt alone and freshly
put here, not herded, not
driven.

TRANSFORMATION

Faithless, we have come here
this morning on empty stomachs
and hearts.
I open my hands to quiet
their stupid pleading, but
they begin to drip
onto the stones.
A woman beside me slips
on those same stones, striking
her head in the Grotto.
Behind me my love with the camera
records it all on color film down
to the finest detail.

But see!
The woman groans, rises slowly
shaking her head: she blesses
those very stones while we escape
through a side door.
Later we play the entire film again and
again. I see the woman keep falling
and getting up, falling and
getting up, Arabs evil-eyeing
the camera. I see myself striking
one pose after the other.

Lord, I tell you
I am without purpose here
in the Holy Land.

My hands grieve in this
bright sunlight.
They walk back and forth along
the Dead Sea shore
with a thirty-year-old man.
Come, Lord. Shrive me.
Too late I hear the film running,
taking it all down.
I look into the camera.
My grin turns to salt. Salt
where I stand.

THREAT

Today a woman signaled me in Hebrew.
Then she pulled out her hair, swallowed it
and disappeared. When I returned home,
shaken, three carts stood by the door with
fingernails showing through the sacks of grain.

CONSPIRATORS

No sleep. Somewhere near here in the woods, fear
envelops the hands of the lookout.

The white ceiling of our room
has lowered alarmingly with dark.

Spiders come out to plant themselves
on every coffee mug.

Afraid? I know if I put out my hand
I will touch an old shoe three inches long
With bared teeth.

Sweetheart, it's time.
I know you're concealed there behind
that innocent handful of flowers.

Come out.
Don't worry, I promise you.

Listen . . .
There is the rap on the door.

But the man who was going to deliver this
instead points a gun at your head.

THIS WORD LOVE

I will not go when she calls
even if she says *I love you,*
especially that,
even though she swears
and promises nothing
but love love.

The light in this room
covers every
thing equally;
even my arm throws no shadow,
it too is consumed with light.

But this word *love*—
this word grows dark, grows
heavy and shakes itself, begins
to eat, to shudder and convulse
its way through this paper
until we too have dimmed in
its transparent throat and still
are riven, are glistening, hip and thigh, your
loosened hair which knows
no hesitation.

DON'T RUN

*Nadya, pink-cheeked, happy, her eyes shining with tears
in expectation of something extraordinary, circled
in the dance, her white dress billowing and showing glimpses
of her slim, pretty legs in their flesh-tinted
stockings. Varya, thoroughly contented, took Podgorin by the arm
and said to him under her breath with significant expression:
"Misha, don't run away from your happiness. Take it
while it offers itself to you freely, later you will be running
after it, but you won't overtake it."*

—ANTON CHEKHOV
"A Visit to Friends"

WOMAN BATHING

Naches River. Just below the falls.
Twenty miles from any town. A day
of dense sunlight
heavy with odors of love.
How long have we?
Already your body, sharpness of Picasso,
is drying in this highland air.
I towel down your back, your hips,
with my undershirt.
Time is a mountain lion.
We laugh at nothing,
and as I touch your breasts
even the ground-
           squirrels
are dazzled.

II

THE NAME

I got sleepy while driving and pulled in under a tree at the side of the road. Rolled up in the back seat and went to sleep. How long? Hours. Darkness had come.

All of a sudden I was awake, and didn't know who I was. I'm fully conscious, but that doesn't help. Where am I? WHO am I? I am something that has just woken up in a back seat, throwing itself around in panic like a cat in a gunnysack. Who am I?

After a long while my life comes back to me. My name comes to me like an angel. Outside the castle walls there is a trumpet blast (as in the Leonora Overture) and the footsteps that will save me come quickly quickly down the long staircase. It's me coming! It's me!

But it is impossible to forget the fifteen-second battle in the hell of nothingness, a few feet from a major highway where the cars slip past with their lights on.

—Tomas Tranströmer
(translated by Robert Bly)

LOOKING FOR WORK

I have always wanted brook trout
for breakfast.

Suddenly, I find a new path
to the waterfall.

I begin to hurry.
Wake up,

my wife says,
you're dreaming.

But when I try to rise,
the house tilts.

Who's dreaming?
It's noon, she says.

My new shoes wait by the door,
gleaming.

THE WORLD BOOK SALESMAN

He holds conversation sacred
though a dying art. Smiling,
by turns he is part toady,
part *Oberführer*. Knowing when
is the secret.
Out of the slim briefcase come
maps of all the world;
                    deserts, oceans,
photographs, artwork—
it is all there, all there
for the asking
as the doors swing open, crack
or slam.

In the empty
rooms each evening, he eats
alone, watches television, reads
the newspaper with a lust
that begins and ends in the fingertips.
There is no God,
and conversation is a dying art.

THE TOES

This foot's giving me nothing
but trouble. The ball,
the arch, the ankle—I'm saying
it hurts to walk. But
mainly it's these toes
I worry about. Those
"terminal digits" as they're
otherwise called. How true!
For them no more delight
in going headfirst
into a hot bath, or
a cashmere sock. Cashmere socks,
no socks, slippers, shoes, Ace
bandage—it's all one and the same
to these dumb toes.
They even looked zonked out
and depressed, as if
somebody'd pumped them full
of Thorazine. They hunch there
stunned and mute—drab, lifeless
things. What in hell is going on?
What kind of toes are these
that nothing matters any longer?
Are these really *my*
toes? Have they forgotten
the old days, what it was like
being alive then? Always first
on line, first onto the dance floor
when the music started.

First to kick up their heels.
Look at them. No, don't.
You don't want to see them,
those slugs. It's only with pain
and difficulty they can recall
the other times, the good times.
Maybe what they really want
is to sever all connection
with the old life, start over,
go underground, live alone
in a retirement manor
somewhere in the Yakima Valley.
But there was a time
they used to strain
with anticipation
simply
curl with pleasure
at the least provocation,
the smallest thing.
The feel of a silk dress
against the fingers, say.
A becoming voice, a touch
behind the neck, even
a passing glance. Any of it!
The sound of hooks being
unfastened, stays coming
undone, garments letting go
onto a cool, hardwood floor.

THE MOON, THE TRAIN

The moon, the landscape, the train.
We are moving steadily along the south shore
of the lake, past the spas and sanitoriums.
The conductor comes through the club car to tell us
that if we look to the left—there, where those
lights are shining—we will see a lighted tennis
court, and it's probable, even at this hour, we'll
find Franz Kafka on the court. He's crazy about
tennis and can't get enough of it. In a minute, sure
enough—there's Kafka, dressed in whites,
playing doubles against a young man and woman.
An unidentified young woman is Kafka's partner. Which
pair is ahead? Who is keeping score? The ball goes back
and forth, back and forth. Everyone seems to be playing perfectly,
intently. None of the players even bothers to look up
at the passing train. Suddenly the track curves
and begins to go through a woods. I turn in the seat
to look back, but either the lights on the court have been
extinguished suddenly, or the train car is in such
a position that everything behind us is darkness.
It is at this moment that all the patrons left in the club car
decide to order another drink, or something to snack on.
Well, and why not? Kafka was a vegetarian and a teetotaler
himself, but that shouldn't crimp anyone's style. Besides,
no one in the train car seems to show the slightest
interest in the game, or who was playing on the court under
the lights. I was going forward to a new and different
life, and I was really only half interested myself, my
thoughts being somewhere else. Nevertheless, I thought it

was something that was of some slight interest and should be pointed out; and I was glad the conductor had done so.

"So that was Kafka," someone behind me spoke up.
"So," somebody else replied. "So what? I'm Perlmutter. Pleased to meet you. Let's have a drink." And saying this, he took a deck of cards out of his shirt pocket and began to shuffle them back and forth on the table in front of him. His huge hands were red and chapped; they seemed to want to devour the cards whole. Once more the track curves and begins to go through a woods.

TWO CARRIAGES

*Again the flying horses, the strange voice of drunken Nicanor,
the wind and the persistent snow which got into one's eyes, one's
mouth, and every fold of one's fur coat. . . . The wind whistled,
the coachmen shouted; and while this frantic uproar was going on,
I recalled all the details of that strange wild day, unique in my
life, and it seemed to me that I really had gone out of my mind
or become a different man. It was as though the man I had been
till that day were already a stranger to me. . . . A quarter of an hour
later his horses fell behind and the sound of his bells were
lost in the roar of the snowstorm.*

—ANTON CHEKHOV
"The Wife"

MIRACLE

They're on a one-way flight, bound from LAX
to SFO, both of them drunk and strung-out
having just squirmed through the hearing,
their second bankruptcy in seven years.
And who knows what, if anything, was said
on the plane, or who said it?
It could have been accumulation
of the day's events, or years on years
of failure and corruption that triggered violence.

Earlier, turned inside out, crucified and left
for dead, they'd been dropped like so much
garbage in front of the terminal. But
once inside they found their bearings,
took refuge in an airport lounge where they tossed
back doubles under a banner that read *Go Dodgers!*
They were plastered, as usual, as they buckled
into their seats and, as always, ready to assume
it was the universal human condition, this battle
waged continually with forces past all reckoning,
forces beyond mere human understanding.

But she's cracking. She can't take any more
and soon, without a word, she turns
in her seat and drills him. Punches him and
punches him, and he takes it.
Knowing deep down he deserves it ten times over—
whatever she wants to dish out—he is being
deservedly beaten for something, there are

good reasons. All the while his head is pummeled,
buffeted back and forth, her fists falling
against his ear, his lips, his jaw, he protects
his whiskey. Grips that plastic glass as if, yes,
it's the long-sought treasure right there
on the tray in front of him.

She keeps on until his nose begins to bleed
and it's then he asks her to stop. *Please, baby,*
for Christ's sake, stop. It may be his plea
reaches her as a faint signal from another
galaxy, a dying star, for this is what it is,
a coded sign from some other time and place
needling her brain, reminding her of something
so lost it's gone forever. In any event, she stops
hitting him, goes back to her drink. Why
does she stop? Because she remembers
the fat years preceding the lean? All that history
they'd shared, sticking it out together, the two
of them against the world? No way. If she'd truly
remembered everything and those years had dropped
smack into her lap all at once,
she would've killed him on the spot.

Maybe her arms are tired, that's why she stops.
Say she's tired then. So she stops. He picks up
his drink almost as if nothing's happened
though it has, of course, and his head aches
and reels with it. She goes back to her whiskey

without a word, not even so much as the usual
"bastard" or "son of a bitch." Dead quiet.
He's silent as lice. Holds the drink
napkin under his nose to catch the blood,
turns his head slowly to look out.

Far below, the small steady lights in houses
up and down some coastal valley. It's
the dinner hour down there. People pushing
up to a full table, grace being said,
hands joined together under roofs so solid
they will never blow off those houses—houses where,
he imagines, decent people live and eat, pray
and pull together. People who, if they left
their tables and looked up from the dining
room windows, could see a harvest moon and,
just below, like a lighted insect, the dim glow
of a jetliner. He strains to see over
the wing and beyond, to the myriad lights
of the city they are rapidly approaching,
the place where they live with others of their kind,
the place they call home.

He looks around the cabin. Other people,
that's all. People like themselves
in a way, male or female, one sex
or the other, people not entirely unlike
themselves—hair, ears, eyes, nose, shoulders,
genitals—my God, even the clothes they wear

are similar, and there's that identifying strap
around the middle. But he knows he and she
are not like those others though he'd like it,
and she too, if they were.

Blood soaks his napkin. His head rings and rings
but he can't answer it. And what would he say
if he could? *I'm sorry they're not in. They left
here, and there too, years ago*. They tear
through the thin night air, belted in, bloody husband
and wife, both so still and pale they could be
dead. But they're not, and that's part of
the miracle. All this is one more giant step
into the mysterious experience of their lives.
Who could have foretold any of it years back when,
their hands guiding the knife, they made
that first cut deep into the wedding cake?
Then the next. Who would have listened?
Anyone bringing such tidings of the future
would have been scourged from the gate.

The plane lifts, then banks sharply. He touches
her arm. She lets him. She even takes his hand.
They were made for each other, right? It's fate.
They'll survive. They'll land and pull themselves
together, walk away from this awful fix—
they simply have to, they must.
There's lots in store for them yet, so many fierce
surprises, such exquisite turnings. It's now

they have to account for, the blood
on his collar, the dark smudge of it
staining her cuff.

MY WIFE

My wife has disappeared along with her clothes.
She left behind two nylon stockings, and
a hairbrush overlooked behind the bed.
I should like to call your attention
to these shapely nylons, and to the strong
dark hair caught in the bristles of the brush.
I drop the nylons into the garbage sack; the brush
I'll keep and use. It is only the bed
that seems strange and impossible to account for.

WINE

Reading a life of Alexander the Great, Alexander
whose rough father, Philip, hired Aristotle to tutor
the young scion and warrior, to put some polish
on his smooth shoulders. Alexander who, later
on the campaign trail into Persia, carried a copy of
The Iliad in a velvet-lined box, he loved that book so
much. He loved to fight and drink, too.
I came to that place in the life where Alexander, after
a long night of carousing, a wine-drunk (the worst kind of drunk—
hangovers you don't forget), threw the first brand
to start a fire that burned Persepolis, capital of the Persian Empire
(ancient even in Alexander's day).
Razed it right to the ground. Later, of course,
next morning—maybe even while the fire roared—he was
remorseful. But nothing like the remorse felt
the next evening when, during a disagreement that turned ugly
and, on Alexander's part, overbearing, his face flushed
from too many bowls of uncut wine, Alexander rose drunkenly to
            his feet,
grabbed a spear and drove it through the breast
of his friend, Cletus, who'd saved his life at Granicus.

For three days Alexander mourned. Wept. Refused food. "Refused
to see to his bodily needs." He even promised
to give up wine forever.
(I've heard such promises and the lamentations that go with them.)
Needless to say, life for the army came to a full stop
as Alexander gave himself over to his grief.
But at the end of those three days, the fearsome heat

beginning to take its toll on the body of his dead friend,
Alexander was persuaded to take action. Pulling himself together
and leaving his tent, he took out his copy of Homer, untied it,
began to turn the pages. Finally he gave orders that the funeral
rites described for Patroklos be followed to the letter:
he wanted Cletus to have the biggest possible send-off.
And when the pyre was burning and the bowls of wine were
passed his way during the ceremony? Of course, what do you
think? Alexander drank his fill and passed
out. He had to be carried to his tent. He had to be lifted, to be put
into his bed.

AFTER THE FIRE

*The little bald old man, General Zhukov's cook, the very one
whose cap had been burnt, walked in. He sat down and
listened. Then he, too, began to reminisce and tell stories.
Nikolay, sitting on the stove with his legs hanging down,
listened and asked questions about the dishes
that were prepared for the gentry in the old days.
They talked about chops, cutlets, various soups and sauces, and
the cook, who remembered everything very well, mentioned dishes
that were no longer prepared; there was one, for instance—a dish
made of bulls' eyes, that was called "waking up
in the morning."*

—ANTON CHEKHOV
"Peasants"

III

from A JOURNAL OF SOUTHERN RIVERS

What lasts is what you start with.

—CHARLES WRIGHT

THE KITCHEN

At Sportsmen's Park, near Yakima, I crammed a hook
with worms, then cast it toward the middle
of the pond, hoping for bass. Bullfrogs scraped the air
invisibly. A turtle, flapjack-sized, slid
from a lily pad while another pulled itself onto
the same pad, a little staging area. Blue sky, warm
afternoon. I pushed a forked branch
into the sandy bank, rested the pole in the fork,
watched the bobber for a while, then beat off.
Grew sleepy then and let my eyes close.
Maybe I dreamed. I did that back then. When
suddenly, in my sleep, I heard a plop, and my eyes
flew open. My pole was gone!
I saw it tearing a furrow through
the scummy water. The bobber appeared, then
disappeared, then showed itself once more
skimming the surface, then gone under again.
What could I do? I bellowed, and bellowed some more.
Began to run along the bank, swearing to God
I would not touch myself again if He'd let me
retrieve that pole, that fish. Of course
there was no answer, not a sign.
I hung around the pond a long time
(the same pond that'd take my friend a year later),
once in a while catching a glimpse of my bobber,
now here, now there. Shadows grew fat
and dropped from trees into the pond. Finally
it was dark, and I biked home.

My dad was drunk
and in the kitchen with a woman not his wife, nor
my mother either. This woman was, I swear, sitting
on his lap, drinking a beer. A woman
with part of a front tooth
missing. She tried to grin as she rose
to her feet. My dad stayed where he was, staring at me
as if he didn't recognize his own get. *Here,*
what is it, boy? he said. *What happened,*
son? Swaying against the sink, the woman wet her lips
and waited for whatever was to happen next.
My dad waited too, there in his old place
at the kitchen table, the bulge in his pants
subsiding. We all waited and wondered
at the stuttered syllables, the words made to cling
as anguish that poured from my raw young mouth.

SONGS IN THE DISTANCE

*Because it was a holiday, they bought a herring at the tavern
and made a soup of the herring head. At midday
they sat down to have tea and went on drinking it until
they were all perspiring: they looked actually swollen with
tea; and then they attacked the soup, all helping themselves
out of one pot. The herring itself Granny hid away.
In the evening a potter was firing pots on the slope. Down
below in the meadow the girls got up a round dance
and sang songs . . . and in the distance the singing sounded soft
and melodious. In and about the tavern the peasants were
making a racket. They sang with drunken voices, discordantly,
and swore at one another. . . . And the girls and children listened
to the swearing without turning a hair; it was evident
that they had been used to it from their cradles.*

—ANTON CHEKHOV
"Peasants"

SUSPENDERS

Mom said I didn't have a belt that fit and
I was going to have to wear suspenders to school
next day. Nobody wore suspenders to second grade,
or any other grade for that matter. She said,
You'll wear them or else I'll use them on you. I don't
want any more trouble. My dad said something then. He
was in the bed that took up most of the room in the cabin
where we lived. He asked if we could be quiet and settle this
in the morning. Didn't he have to go in early to work in
the morning? He asked if I'd bring him
a glass of water. It's all that whiskey he drank, Mom said. He's
dehydrated.

I went to the sink and, I don't know why, brought him
a glass of soapy dishwater. He drank it and said, That sure
tasted funny, son. Where'd this water come from?
Out of the sink, I said.
I thought you loved your dad, Mom said.
I do, I do, I said, and went over to the sink and dipped a glass
into the soapy water and drank off two glasses just
to show them. I love Dad, I said.
Still, I thought I was going to be sick then and there. Mom said,
I'd be ashamed of myself if I was you. I can't believe you'd
do your dad that way. And, by God, you're going to wear those
suspenders tomorrow, or else. I'll snatch you bald-headed if you
give me any trouble in the morning. I don't want to wear
        suspenders,
I said. You're going to wear suspenders, she said. And with that
she took the suspenders and began to whip me around the bare legs

while I danced in the room and cried. My dad
yelled at us to stop, for God's sake, stop. His head was killing him,
and he was sick at his stomach from soapy dishwater
besides. That's thanks to this one, Mom said. It was then somebody
began to pound on the wall of the cabin next to ours. At first it
sounded like it was a fist—*boom-boom-boom*—and then
whoever it was switched to a mop or a broom
handle. For Christ's sake, go to bed over there! somebody yelled.
Knock it off! And we did. We turned out the lights and
got into our beds and became quiet. The quiet that comes to a house
where nobody can sleep.

WHAT YOU NEED TO
KNOW FOR FISHING

*The angler's coat and trowsers should be of cloth,
not too thick and heavy, for if they be the sooner wet
they will be the sooner dry. Water-proof velveteens,
fustians, and mole-skins—rat catcher's costume—
ought never to be worn by the angler for if
he should have to swim a mile or two on any occasion
he would find them a serious weight once thoroughly
saturated with water. And should he have a stone
of fish in his creel, it would be safest not to make
the attempt. An elderly gentleman of my acquaintance
suggests the propriety of anglers wearing* cork *jackets
which, if strapped under the shoulders, would enable
the wearer to visit any part of a lake where,
in warm weather, with an umbrella over his head,
he might enjoy his sport, cool and comfortable, as if
"in a sunny pleasure dome with caves of ice."
This same gentleman thinks that a bottle of* Reading *sauce,
a box of "peptic pills," and a portable frying-pan
ought to form part of every angler's travelling equipage.*

—STEPHEN OLIVER
from *Scenes and Recollections of Fly Fishing in
Northumberland, Cumberland and Westmoreland* (1834)

OYNTMENT TO ALURE
FISH TO THE BAIT

Take Mans Fat and Cats Fat, of each half an Ounce;
Mummy finely poudred, three Drams; Cummin-seed
finely poudred, one Dram; distilled Oyl of Annise
and Spike, of each six Drops; Civet two Grains,
and Camphir four Grains. Make an Oyntment.
When you Angle, annoint eight Inches of the Line
next the Hook therewith, and keep it in
a pewter Box. When you use this Oyntment
never Angle with less than three hairs next Hook
because if you Angle with but one hair
it will not stick on. Take the Bones or Scull
of a Dead-man, at the opening of a Grave,
and beat the same into pouder, and put this pouder
in the Moss wherein you keep your worms. But
others like Grave-earth as well. Now
go find your water.

—JAMES CHETHAM
from *The Angler's Vade Mecum* (1681)

THE STURGEON

Narrow-bodied, iron head like the flat side
of a lance,
        mouth underneath,
the sturgeon is a bottom-feeder
and can't see well.
Mosslike feelers hang down over
the slumbrous lips,
and its dorsal fins and plated backbone
mark it out
something left over from another world.
The sturgeon
lives alone, confines itself
to large, freshwater rivers, and takes
100 years getting around to its first mating.

        Once with my father
at the Central Washington State Fair
I saw a sturgeon that weighed 900 pounds
winched up in a corner
of the Agricultural Exhibit Building.
I will not forget that.
A card gave the name in italics,
also a sketch, as they say,
of its biography—
    which my father read
    and then read aloud.

The largest are netted
in the Don River

somewhere in Russia.
These are called White Sturgeon
and no one can be sure
just how large they are.
The next biggest ones recorded
are trapped at the mouth
of the Yukon River in Alaska
and weigh upwards of 1,900 pounds.

This particular specimen
            —I am quoting—
was killed in the exploratory dynamiting
that went on in the summer of 1951
at Celilo Falls on the Columbia River.
I remember my father told me
a story then about three men he knew long ago in Oregon
who hooked what must have been the largest in the world.
                    So big, he said,
                they fastened a team of horses
                to it—the cable or chain, whatever
                they were using for line—
                and for a while, even the horses
                were at a standstill.

I don't remember much else—
maybe it got away
even then—just my father there beside me
leaning on his arms over the railing, staring, the two of us
staring up at that great dead fish,

and that marvelous story of his, all
surfacing, now and then.

NIGHT DAMPNESS

*I am sick and tired of the river, the stars
that strew the sky, this heavy funereal silence.
To while away the time, I talk to my coachman, who
looks like an old man. . . . He tells me that this dark, forbidding river
abounds in sterlet, white salmon, eel-pout, pike, but there is no one
to catch the fish and no tackle to catch it with.*

—ANTON CHEKHOV
"Across Siberia"

ANOTHER MYSTERY

That time I tagged along with my dad to the dry cleaners—
What'd I know then about Death? Dad comes out carrying
a black suit in a plastic bag. Hangs it up behind the back seat
of the old coupe and says, "This is the suit your grandpa
is going to leave the world in." What on earth
could he be talking about? I wondered.
I touched the plastic, the slippery lapel of that coat
that was going away, along with my grandpa. Those days it was
just another mystery.

Then there was a long interval, a time in which relatives departed
this way and that, left and right. Then it was my dad's turn.
I sat and watched him rise up in his own smoke. He didn't own
a suit. So they dressed him gruesomely
in a cheap sports coat and tie,
for the occasion. Wired his lips
into a smile as if he wanted to reassure us, *Don't worry, it's
not as bad as it looks.* But we knew better. He was dead,
wasn't he? What else could go wrong? (His eyelids
were sewn closed, too, so he wouldn't have to witness
the frightful exhibit.) I touched
his hand. Cold. The cheek where a little stubble had
broken through along the jaw. Cold.

Today I reeled this clutter up from the depths.
Just an hour or so ago when I picked up my own suit
from the dry cleaners and hung it carefully behind the back seat.
I drove it home, opened the car door and
lifted it out into sunlight. I stood there a minute

in the road, my fingers crimped on the wire hanger. Then
tore a hole through the plastic to the other side. Took one of
the empty sleeves between my fingers and held it—
the rough, palpable fabric.
I reached through to the other side.

IV

RETURN TO KRAKÓW IN 1880

So I returned here from the big capitals,
To a town in a narrow valley under the cathedral hill
With royal tombs. To a square under the tower
And the shrill trumpet sounding noon, breaking
Its note in half because the Tartar arrow
Has once again struck the trumpeter.
And pigeons. And the garish kerchiefs of women selling flowers.
And groups chattering under the Gothic portico of the church.
My trunk of books arrived, this time for good.
What I know of my laborious life: it was lived.
Faces are paler in memory than on daguerreotypes.
I don't need to write memos and letters every morning.
Others will take over, always with the same hope,
The one we know is senseless and devote our lives to.
My country will remain what it is, the backyard of empires,
Nursing its humiliation with provincial daydreams.
I leave for a morning walk tapping with my cane:
The places of old people are taken by new old people
And where the girls once strolled in their rustling skirts,
New ones are strolling, proud of their beauty.
And children trundle hoops for more than half a century.
In a basement a cobbler looks up from his bench,
A hunchback passes by with his inner lament,
Then a fashionable lady, a fat image of the deadly sins.
So the Earth endures, in every petty matter

And in the lives of men, irreversible.
And it seems a relief. To win? To lose?
What for, if the world will forget us anyway.

—CZESLAW MILOSZ
(translated by Milosz and Robert Hass)

SUNDAY NIGHT

Make use of the things around you.
This light rain
Outside the window, for one.
This cigarette between my fingers,
These feet on the couch.
The faint sound of rock-and-roll,
The red Ferrari in my head.
The woman bumping
Drunkenly around in the kitchen . . .
Put it all in,
Make use.

THE PAINTER & THE FISH

All day he'd been working like a locomotive.
I mean he was *painting,* the brush strokes
coming like clockwork. Then he called
home. And that was that. That was all she
wrote. He shook like a leaf. He started
smoking again. He lay down and got back
up. Who could sleep if your woman sneered
and said time was running out? He drove
into town. But he didn't go drinking.
No, he went walking. He walked past a mill
called "the mill." Smell of fresh-cut
lumber, lights everywhere, men driving
jitneys and forklifts, driving themselves.
Lumber piled to the top of the warehouse,
the whine and groan of machinery. Easy
enough to recollect, he thought. He went
on, rain falling now, a soft rain that wants
to do its level best not to interfere
with anything and in return asks only
that it not be forgotten. The painter
turned up his collar and said to himself
he wouldn't forget. He came to a lighted
building where, inside a room, men played
cards at a big table. A man wearing
a cap stood at the window and looked
out through the rain as he smoked
a pipe. That was an image he didn't
want to forget either, but then
with his next thought he
shrugged. What was the point?

He walked on until he reached the jetty
with its rotten pilings. Rain fell
harder now. It hissed as it struck
the water. Lightning came and went.
Lightning broke across the sky
like memory, like revelation. Just
when he was at the point of despair,
a fish came up out of the dark
water under the jetty and then fell back
and then rose again in a flash
to stand on its tail and shake itself!
The painter could hardly credit
his eyes, or his ears! He'd just
had a sign—faith didn't enter
into it. The painter's mouth flew
open. By the time he'd reached home
he'd quit smoking and vowed never
to talk on the telephone again.
He put on his smock and picked up
his brush. He was ready to begin
again, but he didn't know if one
canvas could hold it all. Never
mind. He'd carry it over
onto another canvas if he had to.
It was all or nothing. Lightning, water,
fish, cigarettes, cards, machinery,

the human heart, that old port.
Even the woman's lips against
the receiver, even that.
The curl of her lip.

AT NOON

*You are served "duck soup" and nothing more. But you
can hardly swallow this broth; it is a turbid liquid
in which bits of wild duck and guts
imperfectly cleaned are swimming. . . .
It is far from tasty.*

—ANTON CHEKHOV
"Across Siberia"

ARTAUD

Among the hieroglyphs, the masks, the unfinished poems,
the spectacle unfolds: *Antonin et son double.*
They are at work now, calling up the old demons.
The enchantments, etc. The tall, scarred-looking
one at the desk, the one with the cigarette and
no teeth to speak of, is prone to
boldness, to a certain excess
in speech, in gesture. The other is cautious,
watches carefully his opportunity, is effacing even. But
at certain moments still hints broadly, impatiently
of his necessarily arrogant existence.

Antonin, sure enough, there are no more masterpieces.
But your hands trembled as you said it,
and behind every curtain there is always, as you
knew, a rustling.

CAUTION

Trying to write a poem while it was still dark out,
he had the unmistakable feeling he was being watched.
Laid down the pen and looked around. In a minute,
he got up and moved through the rooms of his house.
He checked the closets. Nothing, of course.
Still, he wasn't taking any chances.
He turned off the lamps and sat in the dark.
Smoking his pipe until the feeling had passed
and it grew light out. He looked down
at the white paper before him. Then got up
and made the rounds of his house once more.
The sound of his breathing accompanying him.
Otherwise nothing. Obviously.
Nothing.

ONE MORE

He arose early, the morning tinged with excitement,
eager to be at his desk. He had toast and eggs, cigarettes
and coffee, musing all the while on the work ahead, the hard
path through the forest. The wind blew clouds across
the sky, rattling the leaves that remained on the branches
outside his window. Another few days for them and they'd
be gone, those leaves. There was a poem there, maybe;
he'd have to give it some thought. He went to
his desk, hesitated for a long moment, and then made
what proved to be the most important decision
he'd make all day, something his entire flawed life
had prepared him for. He pushed aside the folder of poems—
one poem in particular still held him in its grip after
a restless night's sleep. (But, really, what's one more, or
less? So what? The work would keep for a while yet,
wouldn't it?) He had the whole wide day opening before him.
Better to clear his decks first. He'd deal with a few items
of business, even some family matters he'd let go far
too long. So he got cracking. He worked hard all day—love
and hate getting into it, a little compassion (very little), some
fellow-feeling, even despair and joy.
There were occasional flashes of anger rising, then
subsiding, as he wrote letters, saying "yes" or "no" or "it
depends"—explaining why, or why not, to people out there
at the margin of his life or people he'd never seen and never
would see. Did they matter? Did they give a damn?
Some did. He took some calls too, and made some others, which
in turn created the need to make a few more. So-and-so, being
unable to talk now, promised to call back next day.

Toward evening, worn out and clearly (but mistakenly, of course)
feeling he'd done something resembling an honest day's work,
he stopped to take inventory and note the couple of
phone calls he'd have to make next morning if
he wanted to stay abreast of things, if he didn't want to
write still more letters, which he didn't. By now,
it occurred to him, he was sick of all business, but he went on
in this fashion, finishing one last letter that should have been
answered weeks ago. Then he looked up. It was nearly dark outside.
The wind had laid. And the trees—they were still now, nearly
stripped of their leaves. But, finally, his desk was clear,
if he didn't count that folder of poems he was
uneasy just to look at. He put the folder in a drawer, out
of sight. That was a good place for it, it was safe there and
he'd know just where to go to lay his hands on it when he
felt like it. Tomorrow! He'd done everything he could do
today. There were still those few calls he'd have to make,
and he forgot who was supposed to call him, and there were a
few notes he was required to send due to a few of the calls,
but he had it made now, didn't he? He was out of the woods.
He could call today a day. He'd done what he had to do.
What his duty told him he should do. He'd fulfilled his sense of
obligation and hadn't disappointed anybody.

But at that moment, sitting there in front of his tidy desk,
he was vaguely nagged by the memory of a poem he'd wanted
to write that morning, and there was that other poem
he hadn't gotten back to either.

So there it is. Nothing much else needs be said, really. What
can be said for a man who chooses to blab on the phone
all day, or else write stupid letters
while he lets his poems go unattended and uncared for, abandoned—
or worse, unattempted. This man doesn't deserve poems
and they shouldn't be given to him in any form.

His poems, should he ever produce any more,
ought to be eaten by mice.

AT THE BIRD MARKET

There is no deceiving the bird-fancier. He sees and understands his bird from a distance. "There is no relying on that bird," a fancier will say,
looking into a siskin's beak, and counting the feathers on its tail. "He sings now, it's true, but what of that? I sing in company too. No, my boy, shout, sing to me without company; sing in solitude, if you can. . . . Give me the quiet one!"

—ANTON CHEKHOV
"The Bird Market"

HIS BATHROBE POCKETS
STUFFED WITH NOTES

Talking about her brother, Morris, Tess said:
"The night always catches him. He never
believes it's coming."

That time I broke a tooth on barbecued ribs.
I was drunk. We were all drunk.

The early sixteenth-century Belgian painter called,
for want of his real name,
"The Master of the Embroidered Leaf."

Begin the novel with the young married couple
getting lost in the woods, just after the picnic.

Those dead birds on the porch when I opened up
the house after being away for three months.

The policeman whose nails were bitten
to the quick.

Aunt Lola, the shoplifter, rolled her own dad
and other drunks as well.

Dinner at Doug and Amy's. Steve ranting, as usual,
about Bob Dylan, the Vietnam War, granulated sugar,
silver mines in Colorado. And, as usual, just
as we sit down the phone rings and is passed around
the table so everyone can say something. (It's Jerry.)
The food grows cold. No one is hungry anyway.

"We've sustained damage, but we're still able
to maneuver." Spock to Captain Kirk.

Remember Haydn's 104 symphonies. Not all of them
were great. But there were 104 of them.

The rabbi I met on the plane that time who gave me comfort
just after my marriage had broken up for good.

Chris's story about going to an AA meeting where
a well-to-do family comes in—"freaked out,"
her words—because they've just been robbed at gunpoint.

Three men and a woman in wet suits. The door to their
motel room is open and they are watching TV.

"I am disbanding the fleet and sending it back
to Macedonian shores." Richard Burton, *Alexander the Great.*

Don't forget when the phone was off the hook
all day, every day.

The bill collector (in Victoria, B.C.) who asks
the widow if she'd like it if the bailiff dug up
her husband and repossessed the suit he was buried in.

"Your bitter grief is proof enough." Mozart,
La Clemenza di Tito, Act II, Scene 2.

The woman in El Paso who wants to give us her furniture.
But it's clear she is having a nervous breakdown.
We're afraid to touch it. Then we take the bed, and a chair.

Duke Ellington riding in the back of his limo, somewhere
in Indiana. He is reading by lamplight. Billy Strayhorn
is with him, but asleep. The tires hiss on the pavement.
The Duke goes on reading and turning the pages.

I've got—how much longer?

Enough horsing around!

THE MARCH INTO RUSSIA

Just when he had given up thinking
he'd ever write another line of poetry,
she began brushing her hair.
And singing that Irish folk song
he liked so much.
That one about Napoleon and
his "bonnie bunch of roses, oh!"

SOME PROSE ON *POETRY*

Years ago—it would have been 1956 or 1957—when I was a teenager, married, earning my living as a delivery boy for a pharmacist in Yakima, a small town in eastern Washington, I drove with a prescription to a house in the upscale part of town. I was invited inside by an alert but very elderly man wearing a cardigan sweater. He asked me to please wait in his living room while he found his checkbook.

There were a lot of books in that living room. Books were everywhere, in fact, on the coffee table and end tables, on the floor next to the sofa—every available surface had become the resting place for books. There was even a little library over against one wall of the room. (I'd never seen a *personal* library before; rows and rows of books arranged on built-in shelves in someone's private residence.) While I waited, eyes moving around, I noticed on his coffee table a magazine with a singular and, for me, startling name on its cover: *Poetry*. I was astounded, and I picked it up. It was my first glimpse of a "little magazine," not to say a poetry magazine, and I was dumbstruck. Maybe I was greedy: I picked up a book, too, something called *The Little Review Anthology,* edited by Margaret Anderson. (I should add that it was a mystery to me then just what "edited by" meant.) I fanned the pages of the magazine and, taking still more liberty, began to leaf through the pages of the book. There were lots of poems in the book, but also prose pieces and what looked like remarks or even pages of commentary on each of the selections. What on earth *was* all this? I wondered. I'd never before seen a book like it—nor, of course, a magazine like *Poetry.* I looked from one to the other of these publications, and secretly coveted each of them.

When the old gentleman had finished writing out his check, he said, as if reading my heart, "Take that book with you, sonny. You might find something in there you'll like. Are you interested in poetry?

Why don't you take the magazine too? Maybe you'll write something yourself someday. If you do, you'll need to know where to send it."

Where to send it. Something—I didn't know just what, but I felt something momentous happening. I was eighteen or nineteen years old, obsessed with the need to "write something," and by then I'd made a few clumsy attempts at poems. But it had never really occurred to me that there might be a place where one actually sent these efforts in hopes they would be read and even, just possibly—incredibly, or so it seemed—considered for publication. But right there in my hand was visible proof that there were responsible people somewhere out in the great world who produced, sweet Jesus, a monthly magazine of poetry. I was staggered. I felt, as I've said, in the presence of revelation. I thanked the old gentleman several times over, and left his house. I took his check to my boss, the pharmacist, and I took *Poetry* and *The Little Review* book home with me. And so began an education.

Of course, I can't recall the names of any of the contributors to that issue of the magazine. Most likely there were a few distinguished older poets alongside new, "unknown" poets, much the same situation that exists within the magazine today. Naturally, I hadn't heard of anyone in those days—or read anything either, for that matter, modern, contemporary or otherwise. I do remember I noted the magazine had been founded in 1912 by a woman named Harriet Monroe. I remember the date because that was the year my father had been born. Later that night, bleary from reading, I had the distinct feeling my life was in the process of being altered in some significant and even, forgive me, magnificent way.

In the anthology, as I recall, there was serious talk about "modernism" in literature, and the role played in advancing modernism by a man bearing the strange name of Ezra Pound. Some of his poems, letters and lists of rules—the do's and don't's for writing—had been included in the anthology. I was told that, early in the life of *Poetry,* this Ezra Pound had served as foreign editor for the magazine—the same magazine which had on that day passed into my hands. Further, Pound had been instrumental in introducing the work of a large number of new poets to Monroe's magazine, as well as to *The Little Review,* of course; he was, as everyone knows, a tireless editor and promoter—poets with names like H. D., T. S. Eliot, James Joyce, Richard Aldington, to cite only a handful. There was discussion and analysis of poetry movements; imagism, I remember, was one of these movements. I learned that, in addition to *The Little Review, Poetry* was one of the magazines hospitable to imagist writing. By then I was reeling. I don't see how I could have slept much that night.

This was back in 1956 or 1957, as I've said. So what excuse is there for the fact that it took me twenty-eight years or more to finally send off some work to *Poetry?* None. The amazing thing, the crucial factor, is that when I did send something, in 1984, the magazine was still around, still alive and well, and edited, as always, by responsible people whose goal it was to keep this unique enterprise running and in sound order. And one of those people wrote to me in his capacity as editor, praising my poems, and telling me the magazine would publish six of them in due course.

Did I feel proud and good about this? Of course I did. And I believe thanks are due in part to that anonymous and lovely old gentleman who gave me his copy of the magazine. Who was he? He would have to be long dead now and the contents of his little library dispersed to wherever small, eccentric, but probably not in the end very valuable collections go—the second-hand bookstores. I'd told him that day I would read his magazine and read the book, too, and I'd get back to him about what I thought. I didn't do that, of course. Too many other things intervened; it was a promise easily given and broken the moment the door closed behind me. I never saw him again, and I don't know his name. I can only say this encounter really happened, and in much the way I've described. I was just a pup then, but nothing can explain, or explain away, such a moment: the moment when the very thing I needed most in my life—call it a polestar—was casually, generously given to me. Nothing remotely approaching that moment has happened since.

POEMS

They've come every day this month.
Once I said I wrote them because
I didn't have time for anything
else. Meaning, of course, better
things—things other than mere
poems and verses. Now I'm writing
them because I want to.
More than anything because
this is February
when normally not much of anything
happens. But this month
the larches have blossomed,
and the sun has come out
every day. It's true my lungs
have heated up like ovens.
And so what if some people
are waiting for the other shoe
to drop, where I'm concerned.
Well, here it is then. Go ahead.
Put it on. I hope it fits
like a shoe.
Close enough, yes, but supple
so the foot has room to breathe
a little. Stand up. Walk
around. Feel it? It will go
where you're going, and be there
with you at the end of your trip.
But for now, stay barefoot. Go
outside for a while, and play.

LETTER

Sweetheart, please send me the notebook I left
on the bedside table. If it isn't *on* the table,
look under the table. Or even under the bed! It's
somewhere. If it isn't a notebook, it's just
a few lines scribbled on some scraps
of paper. But I know it's there. It has to do
with what we heard that time from our doctor friend, Ruth,
about the old woman, eighty-some years old,
"dirty and caked with grime"—the doctor's words—so lacking
in concern for herself that her clothes had stuck
to her body and had to be peeled
from her in the Emergency Room. "I'm so
ashamed. I'm sorry," she kept saying. The smell
of the clothing burned Ruth's eyes! The old woman's fingernails
had grown out and begun to curl in
toward her fingers. She was fighting for breath, her eyes
rolled back in her fright. But she was able, even so, to give
some of her story to Ruth. She'd been a Madison Avenue
debutante, but her father disowned her after
she went to Paris to dance in the Folies Bergère.
Ruth and some of the other Emergency Room staff thought she was
hallucinating. But she gave them the name of her estranged son who
was gay and who ran a gay bar in that same city. He confirmed
everything. Everything the old woman said was true.
Then she suffered a heart attack and died in Ruth's arms.

But I want to see what else I noted from all I heard.
I want to see if it's possible to recreate what it was like
sixty years ago when this young woman stepped off the boat

[73]

in Le Havre, beautiful, poised, determined to make it
on the stage at the Folies Bergère, able
to kick over her head and hop at the same time, to wear feathers
and net stockings, to dance and dance, her arms linked with
the arms of other young women at the Folies Bergère, to high-step it
at the Folies Bergère. Maybe it's
in that notebook with the blue cloth cover, the one
you gave me when we came home from Brazil. I can see
my handwriting next to the name of my winning horse at the track
near the hotel: *Lord Byron*. But the woman, not the dirt, that
doesn't matter, nor even that she weighed nearly 300 pounds.
Memory doesn't care where it lives and mocks
the body. "I understood something about identity once," Ruth
said, recalling her training days, "all of us young medical students
gaping at the hands of a corpse. That's
where the humanness
stays longest—the hands." And the woman's hands. I made a note
at the time, as if I could see them anchored on her
slim hips, the same hands
Ruth let go of, then couldn't forget.

THE YOUNG GIRLS

Forget all experiences involving wincing.
And anything to do with chamber music.
Museums on rainy Sunday afternoons, etcetera.
The old masters. All that.
Forget the young girls. Try and forget them.
The young girls. And all that.

V

from EPILOGUE

Yet why not say what happened?

—ROBERT LOWELL

THE OFFENDING EEL

His former wife called while he was in the south
of France. It was his *chance of a lifetime,*
she suggested, addressing herself
to his answering machine. A celebration
was under way, friends arriving, even as he listened once again
to her voice, confidential yet fortified, too, with
some heady public zeal:

>   *I'm going under fast. But that's not*
>   *the point, that's not why*
>   *I'm calling. I'm telling you, it's a heaven-sent*
>   *opportunity to make a lot of money!*
>   *Call me when you get home for details.*

She hung up, in that distant three weeks ago, then called
right back, unable to contain herself.

>   *Honey, listen. This is not another*
>   *crazy scheme. This, I repeat, is*
>   *the real thing. It's a game*
>   *called Airplane. You start off*
>   *in the economy section then work*
>   *your way forward to the co-pilot's seat,*
>   *or maybe even the pilot's seat!*
>   *You'll get there if*
>   *you're lucky, and you are*
>   *lucky, you always have*
>   *been. You'll make a lot of*
>   *money. I'm not kidding. I'll*
>   *fill you in on details, but you have to*
>   *call me.*

It was sunset, late evening. It was the season

when the grain had begun to head and the fields
were fair with flowers—flowers beginning to nod
as night came on and on, night which really did wear its
"cloak of darkness." Tables were being laid outside; candles
lit and placed in the blossoming pear trees
where, shortly, they would assist the moon
to light the homecoming festivities.

He continued listening to her high, manic voice
on the tape. *Call me,* it said, again and again.
But he wouldn't be calling. He couldn't.
He knew better. They'd been through all that.
His heart which, a few minutes before this message,
had been full and passionate and, for a few minutes anyway,
forgetful and unguarded, shrank in its little place
until it was only a fist-sized muscle joylessly
discharging its duties. What could he do?
She was going to die one of these days and
he was going to die too. This much they knew
and still agreed on. But though many things
had happened in his life, and none more or less
strange than this last-ditch offer of great profit
on her airplane, he'd known for a long time
they would die in separate lives and far from each other,
despite oaths exchanged when they were young.
One or the other of them—she, he felt with dread
certainty—might even die raving, completely
gone off. This seemed a real possibility now.
Anything could happen. What could be done?

Nothing. Nothing, nothing, nothing.
He couldn't even talk to her any longer.
Not only that—he was afraid to. He
deemed her insane. *Call me,* she said.

No, he wouldn't be calling. He stood there,
thinking. Then swerved wildly and remembered
back a couple of days. Finding that passage
in the book as he blasted across the Atlantic
at 1,100 m.p.h., 55,000 feet above it all.
Some young knight riding over the drawbridge
to claim his prize, his bride, a woman he'd never
laid eyes on, one who waited anxiously
inside the keep, combing and combing her long tresses.
The knight rode slowly, splendidly, falcon on his wrist,
gold spurs a-jingle, a sprig of plantagenesta
in his scarlet bonnet. Behind him
many riders, a long row of polished helmets, sun
striking the breastplates of those cavaliers.
Everywhere banners unfurling in the warm breeze,
banners spilling down the high stone walls.

He'd skipped ahead a little and suddenly found
this same man, a prince now, grown disillusioned
and unhappy, possessed of a violent disposition—
drunk, strangling, in the middle of a page,
on a dish of eels. Not a pretty picture.
His cavaliers, who'd also grown coarse
and murderous, they could do nothing except

pound on his back, vainly push greasy fingers
down his throat, vainly hoist him off the floor
by his ankles until he quit struggling.
His face and neck suffused with the colors of sunset.

They let him down then, one of his fingers
still cocked and frozen, aimed at his breast
as if to say *there*. Just there it lodges.
Just over the heart's where this offending eel
can be found. The woman in the story dressed herself
in widow's weeds then dropped from sight, disappeared
into the tapestry. It's true these people
were once real people. But who now remembers?
Tell me, horse, what rider? What banners? What
strange hands unstrapped your bucklers?
Horse, what rider?

SORREL

*Through the open window he could see a flock of ducks
with their young. Waddling and stumbling, they were hurrying
down the road, apparently on their way to the pond. One
duckling picked up a piece of gut that was lying on
the ground, tried to swallow it, choked
on it and raised an alarmed squeaking. Another
duckling ran up, pulled the gut out of its beak and choked on
the thing too. . . . At some distance from the fence,
in the lacy shadow cast on the grass by the young lindens,
the cook Darya was wandering about, picking sorrel
for a vegetable soup.*

—ANTON CHEKHOV
"An Unpleasantness"

THE ATTIC

Her brain is an attic where things
were stored over the years.

From time to time her face appears
in the little windows near the top of the house.

The sad face of someone who has been locked up
and forgotten about.

MARGO

His name was Tug. Hers, Margo.
Until people, seeing what was happening,
began calling her Cargo.
Tug and Cargo. He had drive,
they said. Lots of hair on his face
and arms. A big guy. Commanding
voice. She was more laid-back. A blond.
Dreamy. (Sweet and dreamy.) She broke
loose, finally. Sailed away
under her own power. Went to places
pictured in books, and some
not in any book, or even on the map.
Places she, being a girl, and cargo,
never dreamed of getting to.
Not on her own, anyway.

ON AN OLD PHOTOGRAPH
OF MY SON

It's 1974 again, and he's back once more. Smirking,
a pair of coveralls over a white tee-shirt,
no shoes. His hair, long and blond, falls
to his shoulders like his mother's did
back then, and like one of those young Greek
heroes I was just reading about. But
there the resemblance ends. On his face
the contemptuous expression of the wise guy,
the petty tyrant. I'd know that look anywhere.
It burns in my memory like acid. It's
the look I never hoped I'd live to see
again. I want to forget that boy
in the picture—that jerk, that bully!

What's for supper, mother dear? Snap to!
Hey, old lady, jump, why don't you? Speak
when spoken to. I think I'll put you in
a headlock to see how you like it. I like
it. I want to keep you on
your toes. Dance for me now. Go ahead,
bag, dance. I'll show you a step or two.
Let me twist your arm. Beg me to stop, beg me
to be nice. Want a black eye? You got it!

Oh, son, in those days I wanted you dead
a hundred—no, a thousand—different times.
I thought all that was behind us. Who in hell
took this picture, and
why'd it turn up now,

just as I was beginning to forget?
I look at your picture and my stomach cramps.
I find myself clamping my jaws, teeth on edge, and
once more I'm filled with despair and anger.
Honestly, I feel like reaching for a drink.
That's a measure of your strength and power, the fear
and confusion you still inspire. That's
how mighty you once were. Hey, I hate this
photograph. I hate what became of us all.
I don't want this artifact in my house another hour!
Maybe I'll send it to your mother, assuming
she's still alive somewhere and the post can reach
her this side of the grave. If so, she'll have
a different reaction to it, I know. Your youth and
beauty, that's all she'll see and exclaim over.
My handsome son, she'll say. My boy wonder.
She'll study the picture, searching for her likeness
in the features, and mine. (She'll find them, too.)
Maybe she'll weep, if there are any tears left.
Maybe—who knows?—she'll even wish for those days
back again! Who knows anything anymore?

But wishes don't come true, and it's a good thing.
Still, she's bound to keep your picture out
on the table for a while and make over you
for a time. Then, soon, you'll go
into the big family album along with the other crazies—

herself, her daughter and me, her former husband. You'll be safe in there, cheek to jowl with all your victims. But don't worry, my boy—the pages turn, my son. We all do better in the future.

FIVE O'CLOCK IN THE MORNING

*As he passed his father's room, he glanced in at the door.
Yevgraf Ivanovitch, who had not taken off his clothes or gone
to bed, was standing by the window, drumming on the panes.*

"Goodbye, I am going," said his son.

*"Goodbye . . . the money is on the round table," his father
answered without turning around.*

*A cold, hateful rain was falling as the laborer drove him
to the station. . . . The grass seemed darker than ever.*

—ANTON CHEKHOV
"Difficult People"

SUMMER FOG

To sleep and forget everything for a few hours . . .
To wake to the sound of the foghorn in July.
To look out the window with a heavy heart and see fog
hanging in the pear trees, fog clogging the intersection,
shrouding the neighborhood like a disease invading a healthy
body. To go on living when she has stopped living . . .
    A car eases by with its lights on, and the clock is
turned back to five days ago, the ringing and ringing that brought me
back to this world and news of her death, she who'd simply been
away, whose return had been anticipated with baskets
of raspberries from the market. (Starting from this day
forward, I intend to live my life differently. For one thing,
I won't ever answer the phone again at five in the morning. I knew
better, too, but still I picked up the receiver and said that fateful
word, "Hello." The next time I'll simply let it ring.)
First, though, I have her funeral to get through. It's today, in a
matter of hours. But the idea of a cortege creeping through this fog
to the cemetery is unnerving, and ridiculous, everyone in the town
with their lights on anyway, even the tourists. . . .
    May this fog lift and burn off before three this afternoon! Let us
be able, at least, to bury her under sunny skies, she who worshiped
the sun. Everyone knows she is taking part
in this dark masque today only because she has no choice.
She has lost the power of choice! How she'd
hate this! She who loved in April *deciding*
to plant the sweetpeas and who staked them before
they could climb.

I light my first cigarette of the day and turn away from
the window with a shudder. The foghorn sounds again, filling me
with apprehension, and then, then stupendous
grief.

HUMMINGBIRD
for Tess

Suppose I say *summer,*
write the word "hummingbird,"
put it in an envelope,
take it down the hill
to the box. When you open
my letter you will recall
those days and how much,
just how much, I love you.

OUT

Out of the black mouth of the big king
salmon comes pouring the severed heads of herring,
cut on the bias, slant-wise—
near perfect handiwork of the true
salmon fisherman, him and his slick, sharp bait knife.
Body of the cut herring affixed then eighteen inches behind
a flashing silver spoon, heads tossed over
the side, to sink and turn
in the mottled water. How they managed it, those heads,
to reappear so in our boat—most amazingly!—pouring forth
from the torn mouth, this skewed version, misshapen chunks
of a bad fairy tale, but one where no wishes will be
granted, no bargains struck nor promises kept.

We counted nine of those heads, as if to count was already
to tell it later. "Jesus," you said, "Jesus," before
tossing them back overboard where they belonged.
I started the motor and again we dropped our plugged herring-
baited hooks into the water. You'd been telling stories
about logging for Mormons on Prince of Wales Island (no booze,
no swearing, no women. Just *no,* except for work
and a paycheck). Then you fell quiet, wiped the knife
on your pants and stared toward Canada, and beyond.
All morning you'd wanted to tell me something and now you
began to tell me; how
your wife wants you out of her life, wants
you gone, wants you to just disappear.
Why don't you disappear and just don't ever

come back? she'd said. "Can you beat it? I think she hopes
a spar will take me out." Just then there's one hell of a strike.
The water boils as line goes out. It keeps
going out.

DOWNSTREAM

At noon we have rain, which washes away the snow,
and at dusk, when I stand on the river bank and watch
the approaching boat contend with the current,
a mixture of rain and snow comes down. . . . We go downstream,
keeping close to a thicket of purple willow shrubs. The men
at the oars tell us that only ten minutes ago a boy in a cart
saved himself from drowning by catching hold of
a willow shrub; his team went under. . . .
The bare willow shrubs bend toward the water with
a rustling sound, the river suddenly grows dark. . . . If
there is a storm we shall have to spend the night among
the willows and in the end get drowned, so why not go on?
We put the matter to a vote and decide to row on.

—ANTON CHEKHOV
"Across Siberia"

THE NET

Toward evening the wind changes. Boats
still out on the bay
head for shore. A man with one arm
sits on the keel of a rotting-away
vessel, working on a glimmering net.
He raises his eyes. Pulls at something
with his teeth, and bites hard.
I go past without a word.
Reduced to confusion
by the variableness of this weather,
the importunities of my heart. I keep
going. When I turn back to look
I'm far enough away
to see that man caught in a net.

NEARLY

The two brothers, Sleep and Death, they unblinkingly called
themselves, arrived at our house around nine in the evening, just as
the light was fading. They unloaded all their paraphernalia
in the driveway, what they'd need for killing bees, hornets—yellow-
jackets as well. A "dusky" job, one had said on the phone. Those
invaders, we told ourselves, had become such a nuisance.
Frightening, too. An end to it! And *them,* we decided: we'll write
finish to their short-lived career as pollen-gatherers, honey-
makers. Not a decision taken lightly, or easily. Annihilation on such
an undreamt-of scale, a foreign thing to us. We moved

to the window to look down to the drive where the men, one older,
one younger, stood smoking, watching a few late stragglers find
their way to the hole under the eave. Those bees trying to
beat the sun as it tipped over the horizon, the air turning colder now,
the light gradually fainter. We raised our eyes and, through the
glass, could see a dozen, two dozen, a tiny fist
of them, waiting in a swirl their turn to enter their newfound
city. We could hear rustling, like scales, like wings chaffing
behind the wall, up near the ceiling. Then the sun disappeared

entirely, it was dark. All bees inside. One of the brothers, Sleep, it
must have been, he was the younger, positioned the ladder
in the drive, under the southwest corner. A few words we couldn't
catch were exchanged, then Death pulled on his oversized gloves and
began his climb up the ladder, slowly, balancing on his back
a heavy cannister held papoose-like by a kind of harness. In one hand
was a hose, for killing. He passed our lighted window on his way up,

glancing briefly, incuriously, into the living room. Then he stopped,
about even with our heads, only his boots showing where he stood on
a rung of the ladder. We tried to act as if nothing out of

the ordinary were happening. You picked up a book, sat in your
favorite chair, pretended to concentrate. I put on a record. It was
dark out, darker, as I've said, but there remained a saffron flush in
the western sky, like blood just under the skin. Saffron, that hoarded

spice you said drove the harvesters in Kashmir nearly mad, the
fields ripe with the smell of it. An ecstasy, you said. You turned a
page, as if you'd read a page. The record played and
played. Then came the hiss-hiss of spray as Death pressed
the trigger of his device again and again and again. From the drive
below, Sleep called up, "Give it to them some more, those
bastards." And then, "That's good. That ought to do it, by God. Come
down now." Pretty soon they left, those slicker-coated men, and we

never had to see them or talk to them again. You took a glass of
wine. I smoked a cigarette. That domestic sign mingling with
the covetous reek that hung like a vapor near the cast-iron stove.
What an evening! you said, or I said. We never spoke of it after that.
It was as if something shameful had occurred.
Deep in the night, still awake as the house sailed west, tracking
the moon, we came together in the dark like knives, like wild
animals, fiercely, drawing blood even—something we referred to
next morning as "love-making." We didn't tell each other of our

dreams. How could we? But once in the night, awake, I heard the house creak, almost a sigh, then creak again. Settling, I think it's called.

VI
FOREBODING

"I have a foreboding. . . . *I'm oppressed
by a strange, dark foreboding. As though
the loss of a loved one awaited me."*
  "Are you married, Doctor? You have a family?"
  *"Not a soul. I'm alone, I haven't even any
friends. Tell me, madam, do you believe in forebodings?"*
  "Oh, yes, I do."

—ANTON CHEKHOV
"Perpetuum Mobile"

QUIET NIGHTS

I go to sleep on one beach,
wake up on another.

Boat all fitted out,
tugging against its rope.

SPARROW NIGHTS

*There are terrible nights with thunder, lightning, rain, and
wind, such as are called among the people "sparrow nights."
There has been one such night in my personal life. . . .*

*I woke up after midnight and leaped suddenly out of bed.
It seemed to me for some reason that I was just immediately
going to die. Why did it seem so? I had no sensation
in my body that suggested any immediate death, but my soul
was oppressed with terror, as though I had suddenly seen
a vast menacing glow of fire.*

*I rapidly struck a light, drank some water straight out of
the decanter, then hurried to the open window.
The weather outside was magnificent.
There was a smell of hay and some other
very sweet scent. I could see the spikes of the fence,
the gaunt, drowsy trees by the window, the road,
the dark streak of woodland,
there was a serene, very bright moon in the sky and not a single
cloud, perfect stillness, not one
leaf stirring. I felt that everything was looking at me and
waiting for me to die. . . . My spine was
cold; it seemed to be drawn
inwards, and I felt as though death
were coming upon me stealthily from behind. . . .*

—ANTON CHEKHOV
"A Dreary Story"

LEMONADE

When he came to my house months ago to measure
my walls for bookcases, Jim Sears didn't look like a man
who'd lose his only child to the high waters
of the Elwha River. He was bushy-haired, confident,
cracking his knuckles, alive with energy, as we
discussed tiers, and brackets, and this oak stain
compared to that. But it's a small town, this town,
a small world here. Six months later, after the bookcases
have been built, delivered and installed, Jim's
father, a Mr. Howard Sears, who is "covering for his son"
comes to paint our house. He tells me—when I ask, more
out of small-town courtesy than anything, "How's Jim?"—
that his son lost Jim Jr. in the river last spring.
Jim blames himself. "He can't get over it,
neither," Mr. Sears adds. "Maybe he's gone on to lose
his mind a little too," he adds, pulling on the bill
of his Sherwin-Williams cap.
   Jim had to stand and watch as the helicopter
grappled with, then lifted, his son's body from the river
with tongs. "They used like a big pair of kitchen tongs
for it, if you can imagine. Attached to a cable. But God always
takes the sweetest ones, don't He?" Mr. Sears says. "He has
His own mysterious purposes." "What do *you* think about it?"
I want to know. "I don't want to think," he says. "We
can't ask or question His ways. It's not for us to know.
I just know He taken him home now, the little one."

He goes on to tell me Jim Sr.'s wife took him to thirteen foreign
countries in Europe in hopes it'd help him get over it. But

it didn't. He couldn't. "Mission unaccomplished," Howard says.
Jim's come down with Parkinson's disease. What next?
He's home from Europe now, but still blames himself
for sending Jim Jr. back to the car that morning to look for
that thermos of lemonade. They didn't need any lemonade
that day! Lord, lord, what was he thinking of, Jim Sr. has said
a hundred—no, a thousand—times now, and to anyone who will
still listen. If only he hadn't made lemonade in the first
place that morning! What could he have been thinking about?
Further, if they hadn't shopped the night before at Safeway, and
if that bin of yellowy lemons hadn't stood next to where they
kept the oranges, apples, grapefruit and bananas.
That's what Jim Sr. had really wanted to buy, some oranges
and apples, not lemons for lemonade, forget lemons, he hated
lemons—at least now he did—but Jim Jr., he liked lemonade,
always had. He wanted lemonade.

"Let's look at it this way," Jim Sr. would say, "those lemons
had to come from someplace, didn't they? The Imperial Valley,
probably, or else over near Sacramento, they raise lemons
there, right?" They had to be planted and irrigated and
watched over and then pitched into sacks by field workers and
weighed and then dumped into boxes and shipped by rail or
truck to this god-forsaken place where a man can't do anything
but lose his children! Those boxes would've been off-loaded
from the truck by boys not much older than Jim Jr. himself.
Then they had to be uncrated and poured all yellow and
lemony-smelling out of their crates by those boys, and washed
and sprayed by some kid who was still living, walking around town,

living and breathing, big as you please. Then they were carried
into the store and placed in that bin under that eye-catching sign
that said Have You Had Fresh Lemonade Lately? As Jim Sr.'s
reckoning went, it harks all the way back to first causes, back to
the first lemon cultivated on earth. If there hadn't been any lemons
on earth, and there hadn't been any Safeway store, well, Jim would
still have his son, right? And Howard Sears would still have his
grandson, sure. You see, there were a lot of people involved
in this tragedy. There were the farmers and the pickers of lemons,
the truck drivers, the big Safeway store. . . . Jim Sr., too, he was ready
to assume his share of responsibility, of course. He was the most
guilty of all. But he was still in his nosedive, Howard Sears
told me. Still, he had to pull out of this somehow and go on.
Everybody's heart was broken, right. Even so.

Not long ago Jim Sr.'s wife got him started in a little
wood-carving class here in town. Now he's trying to whittle bears
and seals, owls, eagles, seagulls, anything, but
be can't stick to any one creature long enough to finish
the job, is Mr. Sears's assessment. The trouble is, Howard Sears
goes on, every time Jim Sr. looks up from his lathe, or his
carving knife, he sees his son breaking out of the water downriver,
and rising up—being reeled in, so to speak—beginning to turn and
turn in circles until he was up, way up above the fir trees, tongs
sticking out of his back, and then the copter turning and swinging
upriver, accompanied by the roar and whap-whap of
the chopper blades. Jim Jr. passing now over the searchers who
line the bank of the river. His arms are stretched out from his sides,
and drops of water fly out from him. He passes overhead once more,

closer now, and then returns a minute later to be deposited, ever
so gently laid down, directly at the feet of his father. A man
who, having seen everything now—his dead son rise from the river
in the grip of metal pinchers and turn and turn in circles flying
above the tree line—would like nothing more now than
to just die. But dying is for the sweetest ones. And he remembers
sweetness, when life was sweet, and sweetly
he was given that other lifetime.

SUCH DIAMONDS

*It was a glorious morning. The sun was shining brightly and
cleaving with its rays the layers of white snow
still lingering here and there. The snow as it took leave of
the earth glittered with such diamonds that it hurt the eyes
to look, while the young winter corn was hastily thrusting up
its green beside it. The rooks floated with dignity over
the fields. A rook would fly, drop
to earth, and give several hops before standing firmly
on its feet. . . .*

—ANTON CHEKHOV
"A Nightmare"

WAKE UP

In June, in the Kyborg Castle, in the canton
of Zurich, in the late afternoon, in the room
underneath the chapel, in the dungeon,
the executioner's block hunches on the floor next
to the Iron Maiden in her iron gown. Her serene features
are engraved with a little noncommittal smile. If
you ever once slipped inside her she closed her spiked
interior on you like a demon, like one
possessed. Embrace—that word on the card next to
the phrase "no escape from."
      Over in a corner stands the rack, a dreamlike
contrivance that did all it was called on to do, and more,
no questions asked. And if the victim passed out
too soon from pain, as his bones were being broken
one by one, the torturers simply threw a bucket of water
on him and woke him up. Woke him again,
later, if necessary. They were thorough. They knew
what they were doing.
      The bucket is gone, but there's an old cherrywood
crucifix up on the wall in a corner of the room:
Christ hanging on his cross, of course, what else?
The torturers were human after all, yes? And who
knows—at the last minute their victim might see
the light, some chink of understanding, even acceptance of
his fate might break, might pour into his nearly molten
heart. *Jesu Christo, my Savior.*
      I stare at the block. Why not? Why not indeed?
Who hasn't ever wanted to stick his neck out without fear

of consequence? Who hasn't wanted to lay his life on the line,
then draw back at the last minute?
Who, secretly, doesn't lust after every experience?
It's late. There's nobody else in the dungeon but us,
she and me, the North Pole and the South. I drop down
to my knees on the stone floor, grasp my hands behind
my back, and lay my head on the block. Inch it forward
into the pulse-filled groove until my throat fits the shallow
depression. I close my eyes, draw a breath. A deep breath.
The air thicker somehow, as if I can almost taste it.
For a moment, calm now, I feel I could almost drift off.

    Wake up, she says, and I do, turn my head over to see
her standing above me with her arms raised. I see the axe too,
the one she pretends to hold, so heavy it's all she
can do to hold it up over her shoulder. Only kidding,
she says, and lowers her arms, and the idea-of-axe, then
grins. I'm not finished yet, I say. A minute later, when I
do it again, put my head back down on the block, in
the same polished groove, eyes closed, heart racing
a little now, there's no time for the prayer forming in my
throat. It drops unfinished from my lips as I hear her
sudden movement. Feel flesh against my flesh as the sharp
wedge of her hand comes down unswervingly to the base of
my skull and I tilt, nose over chin into the last
of sight, of whatever sheen or rapture I can grasp to take
with me, wherever I'm bound.

    You can get up now, she says, and
I do. I push myself up off my knees, and I look at her,

neither of us smiling, just shaky
and not ourselves. Then her smile and my arm going
around her hips as we walk into the next corridor
needing the light. And outside then, in the open, needing more.

WHAT THE DOCTOR SAID

He said it doesn't look good
he said it looks bad in fact real bad
he said I counted thirty-two of them on one lung before
I quit counting them
I said I'm glad I wouldn't want to know
about any more being there than that
he said are you a religious man do you kneel down
in forest groves and let yourself ask for help
when you come to a waterfall
mist blowing against your face and arms
do you stop and ask for understanding at those moments
I said not yet but I intend to start today
he said I'm real sorry he said
I wish I had some other kind of news to give you
I said Amen and he said something else
I didn't catch and not knowing what else to do
and not wanting him to have to repeat it
and me to have to fully digest it
I just looked at him
for a minute and he looked back it was then
I jumped up and shook hands with this man who'd just given me
something no one else on earth had ever given me
I may even have thanked him habit being so strong

LET'S ROAR, YOUR HONOR

To *scream with pain, to cry, to summon help, to call*
generally—all that is described here as "roaring."
In Siberia not only bears roar, but sparrows and mice as well.
"The cat got it, and it's roaring," they say of a mouse.

—ANTON CHEKHOV
"Across Siberia"

PROPOSAL

I ask her and then she asks me. We each
accept. There's no back and forth about it. After nearly eleven years
together, we know our minds and more. And this postponement, it's
ripened too. Makes sense now. I suppose we should be
in a rose-filled garden or at least on a beautiful cliff overhanging
the sea, but we're on the couch, the one where sleep
sometimes catches us with our books open, or
some old Bette Davis movie unspools
in glamorous black and white—flames in the fireplace dancing
menacingly in the background as she ascends the marble
staircase with a sweet little snub-nosed
revolver, intending to snuff her ex-lover, the fur coat
he bought her draped loosely over her shoulders. Oh lovely, oh lethal
entanglements. In such a world
to be true.

A few days back some things got clear
about there not being all those years ahead we'd kept
assuming. The doctor going on finally about "the shell" I'd be
leaving behind, doing his best to steer us away from the veil of
tears and foreboding. "But he loves his life," I heard a voice say.
Hers. And the young doctor, hardly skipping a beat, "I know.
I guess you have to go through those seven stages. But you end
up in acceptance."

After that we went to lunch in a little café we'd never
been in before. She had pastrami. I had soup. A lot
of other people were having lunch too. Luckily
nobody we knew. We had plans to make, time pressing down

on us like a vise, squeezing out hope to make room for
the everlasting—that word making me want to shout "Is there
an Egyptian in the house?"

Back home we held on to each other and, without
embarrassment or caginess, let it all reach full meaning. This
was it, so any holding back had to be stupid, had to be
insane and meager. How many ever get to this? I thought
at the time. It's not far from here to needing
a celebration, a joining, a bringing of friends into it,
a handing out of champagne and
Perrier. "Reno," I said. "Let's go to Reno and get married."
In Reno, I told her, it's marriages
and remarriages twenty-four hours a day seven days a week. No
waiting period. Just "I do." And "I do." And if you slip
the preacher ten bucks extra, maybe he'll even furnish
a witness. Sure, she'd heard all

those stories of divorcees tossing their wedding rings into
the Truckee River and marching up to the altar ten minutes later
with someone new. Hadn't she thrown her own last wedding band
into the Irish Sea? But she agreed. Reno was just
the place. She had a green cotton dress I'd bought her in Bath.
She'd send it to the cleaners.
We were getting ready, as if we'd found an answer to
that question of what's left
when there's no more hope: the muffled sound of dice coming down
the felt-covered table, the click of the wheel,
the slots ringing on into the night, and one more, one
more chance. And then that suite we engaged for.

CHERISH

From the window I see her bend to the roses
holding close to the bloom so as not to
prick her fingers. With the other hand she clips, pauses and
clips, more alone in the world
than I had known. She won't
look up, not now. She's alone
with roses and with something else I can only think, not
say. I know the names of those bushes

given for our late wedding: Love, Honor, Cherish—
this last the rose she holds out to me suddenly, having
entered the house between glances. I press
my nose to it, draw the sweetness in, let it cling—scent
of promise, of treasure. My hand on her wrist to bring her close,
her eyes green as river-moss. Saying it then, against
what comes: *wife,* while I can, while my breath, each hurried petal
can still find her.

GRAVY

No other word will do. For that's what it was. Gravy.
Gravy, these past ten years.
Alive, sober, working, loving and
being loved by a good woman. Eleven years
ago he was told he had six months to live
at the rate he was going. And he was going
nowhere but down. So he changed his ways
somehow. He quit drinking! And the rest?
After that it was *all* gravy, every minute
of it, up to and including when he was told about,
well, some things that were breaking down and
building up inside his head. "Don't weep for me,"
he said to his friends. "I'm a lucky man.
I've had ten years longer than I or anyone
expected. Pure gravy. And don't forget it."

NO NEED

I see an empty place at the table.
Whose? Who else's? Who am I kidding?
The boat's waiting. No need for oars
or a wind. I've left the key
in the same place. You know where.
Remember me and all we did together.
Now, hold me tight. That's it. Kiss me
hard on the lips. There. Now
let me go, my dearest. Let me go.
We shall not meet again in this life,
so kiss me goodbye now. Here, kiss me again.
Once more. There. That's enough.
Now, my dearest, let me go.
It's time to be on the way.

THROUGH THE BOUGHS

Down below the window, on the deck, some ragged-looking
birds gather at the feeder. The same birds, I think,
that come every day to eat and quarrel. *Time was, time was,*
they cry and strike at each other. It's nearly time, yes.
The sky stays dark all day, the wind is from the west and
won't stop blowing. . . . Give me your hand for a time. Hold on
to mine. That's right, yes. Squeeze hard. Time was we
thought we had time on our side. *Time was, time was,*
those ragged birds cry.

AFTER-GLOW

The dusk of evening comes on. Earlier a little rain
had fallen. You open a drawer and find inside
the man's photograph, knowing he has only two years
to live. He doesn't know this, of course,
that's why he can mug for the camera.
How could he know what's taking root in his head
at that moment? If one looks to the right
through boughs and tree trunks, there can be seen
crimson patches of the after-glow. No shadows, no
half-shadows. It is still and damp. . . .
The man goes on mugging. I put the picture back
in its place along with the others and give
my attention instead to the after-glow along the far ridge,
light golden on the roses in the garden.
Then, I can't help myself, I glance once more
at the picture. The wink, the broad smile,
the jaunty slant of the cigarette.

LATE FRAGMENT

And did you get what
you wanted from this life, even so?
I did.
And what did you want?
To call myself beloved, to feel myself
beloved on the earth.

ACKNOWLEDGMENTS

Acknowledgment is gratefully given to the following magazines, in which some of the poems in this book originally appeared:

Caliban: "His Bathrobe Pockets Stuffed with Notes"; *Frank:* "Miracle"; *Granta:* "What the Doctor Said"; *Harper's:* "Proposal"; *Hayden's Ferry Review:* "One More," "Cherish"; *Michigan Quarterly Review:* "Wake Up," "Letter"; *Poetry:* "The Net," "Margo," "The Toes," "Wake Up," "Another Mystery," "No Need," "Hummingbird"; *Zyz-zyva:* "The Moon, The Train."

"Gravy" and "After-glow" originally appeared in *The New Yorker.*

"Some Prose on *Poetry*" first appeared in *Poetry,* October–November 1987.

Several poems have also been reprinted from *Near Klamath,* 1968, English Club of Sacramento State College; *Winter Insomnia,* 1970, Kayak Press; *At Night the Salmon Move,* 1976, Capra Press; and *Those Days: Early Writings by Raymond Carver,* 1987, a limited edition published by Raven Editions. These include: "The World Book Salesman," "Artaud," "Woman Bathing," "Transformation," "Threat," "Looking for Work," "Conspirators," "This Word Love," "In a Greek Orthodox Church near Daphne," "The Sturgeon," "My Wife," "Two Worlds."

"His Bathrobe Pockets Stuffed with Notes" was published in a limited edition by Raven Editions, 1988.

"The Painter & the Fish" and "The Toes" were published in limited editions by William B. Ewert, 1988.

"Don't Run," "After the Fire," "Songs in the Distance," "Night Dampness," "At Noon," "Sorrel," "Downstream," "Foreboding," and "Let's Roar, Your Honor" are excerpted from *The Unknown Chekhov,* translated by Avrahm Yarmolinsky. Copyright 1954 by Avrahm Yarmolinsky. Renewal copyright 1982 by Babette Deutsch Yarmolinsky. Reprinted by permission of Farrar, Straus & Giroux.

Excerpt from "Ward No. 6" from *The Horse Stealers and Other Stories* by Anton Chekhov, translated by Constance Garnett. Copyright 1921 by The Macmillan Company, renewed 1949 by David Garnett. Reprinted by permission of Macmillan Publishing Company.

ABOUT THE AUTHOR

Raymond Carver was born in Clatskanie, Oregon, in 1938. *A New Path to the Waterfall* is his eleventh book; his work has also been published in numerous chapbooks and limited editions. He was a Guggenheim Fellow in 1979 and was twice awarded grants from the National Endowment for the Arts. In 1983 Carver received the prestigious Mildred and Harold Strauss Living Award, and in 1985 *Poetry* magazine's Levinson Prize. In 1988 he was elected to the American Academy and Institute of Arts and Letters and was awarded a Doctorate of Letters from the University of Hartford.

A NOTE ON THE TYPE

This book was set in Bembo, a typeface named for Pietro Bembo, the scholar who first used the new typeface in a pamphlet. Bembo was brought into use in 1495 by Aldus Manutius, who became known as the father of modern book production for his printing of well-edited and printed books for the masses.

The Bembo of 1495 was more regular in its appearance than previous roman faces. It is the origin of many roman type styles now classified as "old style" and is characterized by oblique top serifs and horizontal cross-strokes.